Knowledge Management and Intellectual Capital Excellence Awards 2015

An Anthology of Case Histories

Edited by Dan Remenyi

Knowledge Management and Intellectual Capital Excellence Awards 2015:
An Anthology of Case Histories

ISBN: 978-1-910810-52-1

Printed by Lightning Source POD

Published by: Academic Conferences and Publishing International Limited,
Reading, RG4 9SJ, United Kingdom, info@academic-publishing.org

Available from www.academic-bookshop.com

Contents

Acknowledgements

We would like to thank the judges, who initially read the abstracts of the case histories submitted to the competition and discussed these to select those to be submitted as full case histories. They subsequently evaluated the entries and made further selections to produce the finalists who are represented in this book.

Dr Maurizio Massaro

Maurizio has been aggregate professor at Udine University since 2008, having worked as a teacher at Udine University since 2001. He was visiting scholar at the GCU, Florida, USA, in 2010 and at Leicester University in the UK in 2013. His academic interests are primarily in the field of business performance measurement, intellectual capital, knowledge management and entrepreneurship.

Dr Meliha Handzic

Meliha is Professor of Management and Information Systems at the International Burch University, Sarajevo and Suleyman Sah University, Istanbul. Her PhD is from the University of New South Wales, Sydney. Meliha's main research interests lie in the areas of knowledge management and decision support. She has published extensively on these topics in leading journals.

Dr John Dumay

John is Associate Professor in Accounting at Macquarie University, Sydney. Originally a consultant he joined academia after completing his award winning PhD in 2008. John's research specialties are intellectual capital, knowledge management, non-financial reporting, management control, research methodologies and academic writing. John has published over 30 peer reviewed articles in leading academic journals.

Göran Roos

Göran is a founder and recognised world expert of intellectual capital and a major contributor to policy and practice in strategy, innovation, and industrial management. He currently chairs the Advanced Manufacturing Council in Adelaide, and has several economic advisory roles and Professorships at Australian and international institutions. He also worked as a consultant and manager in more than 50 countries. Göran is author/co-author of over one hundred books, chapters, and articles, and is on the editorial boards of the International Journal of Strategic Change Management; the International Journal of Learning and Intellectual Capital and the Journal of Intellectual Capital.

Preface

Although it is only a few decades since knowledge management was thought of as some sort of management fad it has shown itself not to be so. Whereas management fads tend to last for a decade or may be even two, knowledge management can trace its roots back at least half a century.

Knowledge management is now firmly established as an important element in managing the track record of research and teaching. Most universities nowadays have knowledge management courses, as well as academics and students who are interested in research in this field.

However, despite the popularity of knowledge management, and its unquestionable success, there are not many readily accessible examples available of how it has been applied to achieve excellent results for organisations and people. It was for this reason that Academic Conferences and Publishing International decided to create the Knowledge Management and Intellectual Capital Excellence Awards, which runs alongside the European Conference on Knowledge Management. The awards are based on case histories which describe examples of successful applications of knowledge management principles. A panel of experts was established and a call for case histories was announced. The competition was open to academics and practitioners and the examples to be described could be in the university environment, business or industry, government departments or schools etc.

The call for case histories was announced in 2014 and 90 submissions were received, describing on an outline basis what was achieved with these applications of knowledge management principles. There were 70 interesting examples described in these abstracts which were invited to forward a completed case history. The panel of experts then chose 8 case history finalists who were invited to present their work at the 16th annual European Conference on Knowledge management at the University of Udine in the region of Friuli-Venezia Giulia (near Venice), Italy in September 2015.

As can be seen from the Contents page the topics presented range widely, as was expected when working with a subject like Knowledge Management. It may also be observed that the entrants come from many different parts of the world. The competition requires the 3 best to be chosen and it is clear that the judges will have a challenging task to select the winners.

Dr Dan Remenyi

Editor

August 2015

Road Map to Growth and Exit: Jumpstarting Growth with IC

Mary Adams
Smarter-Companies, USA
adams@smarter-companies.com

Abstract

This paper describes an intangible capital (IC) assessment project at a software and services company. In the year prior to the project, the company experienced a small decline in annual revenue on the heels of ten years of rapid growth. This caused concern among the owner/managers. The company initiated this project to create a road map to spark new growth and also to think about how to build the long-term value of this privately-held company.

The project used an IC assessment as an initial diagnostic of the key drivers of growth and value. The main project steps were:

- Workshop with management team to identify the company's unique IC portfolio
- Customization of a standard questionnaire to include these unique IC elements
- Interviews of a 360-degree stakeholder sample that included managers, employees, customers and partners.
- Presentation of findings to the team
- Collaborative creation of an initiative road map
- Design and implementation of key initiatives to effect change
- Design of a set of more traditional metrics to monitor progress

The project used generic tools for survey data gathering, analysis and presentation. The use of IC language was very limited; rather than talk about human capital, for example, the focus was on employees and managers. The data were compelling enough to prompt a series of clear initiatives that did indeed spark a 27% increase in revenues in a little over a year. The principal challenges involved the design of a metric set to monitor the progress of the initiatives; it was hard to find KPI's that gave as clear a read as the qualitative assessments.

This project became the foundation for tools that have since been used in a couple dozen other companies. The next step for the methodology is to more fully automate the assessment process and move from a model of assessment at a moment in time to a continuous on-line communication with stakeholders.

1   Introduction

This project took place at a software and services company that had grown steadily for the first ten years of its operations but had then lost momentum and experienced a small decline in revenue. This caused concern among the owner/managers. They engaged an outside consulting firm to help them regain momentum. The goal of the project was to create a road map to spark growth once again and also to think about how to build the long-term value of this privately-held company.

2   Infrastructure

The main infrastructure of this initiative was a consulting and assessment methodology developed by the partners of the consulting firm. Having the partners involved in this project was helpful although in later projects, other consultants with less experience with the approach were able to implement the methodology successfully.

The key project phases were:

A.   Project design
B.   Assessment
C.   Planning
D.   Execution
E.   Measurement and Reporting

It's important to point out that while this project drew heavily on intellectual or intangible capital (IC) theory, the purpose of the project was not IC in itself. IC was a means to an end and was not discussed in depth during the project design. Rather, the language used focused on "value drivers." These drivers were identified, for example, as elements like employees and management (rather than human capital) and processes and technology (rather than structural capital). Conversations with company management validated that the IC elements were highly relevant to them even though they were not familiar with the IC theory and language. IC reflected their reality as a growing software and services company dependent on knowledge as a competitive advantage.

The assessment phase progressed as follows:

1. Workshop with senior team to identify the company's core IC
2. Customization of a standard questionnaire to include these unique IC elements
3. Identification of stakeholder sample
4. Interviews of stakeholders by consulting team using the questionnaire
5. Report preparation
6. Presentation of findings to the team and launch of the Planning Step

The questionnaire used in the assessment phase was developed by the consulting firm and included 66 questions in all that were divided into four categories and ten subcategories using an IC framework:

- Human Capital – Management and Employees
- Structural Capital – Processes and Systems, Technology, and Marketing and Sales
- Relationship Capital – Customer Base, Partnerships, Brand
- Strategic Capital – Business Model, External Factors

Of the 66 questions, 38 (58%) were customized to the company using the inventory depicted in Figure 1. For example, the questions about employees included five core competencies that are critical to the value creation system of the company. In a similar manner, questions about five processes and four key categories of external partnerships were also included in the instrument based on the inventory. This was an important aspect of the project plan because it ensured that the questions (and answers) were highly relevant to all involved.

PEERS	Software providers to hospitals				
BRAND(S) [Company Name]	**CUSTOMERS** IT departments of middle market hospitals in the U.S.	**VALUE PROPOSITION** Ensure that the 50-75 software packages running in the average hospital work seamlessly together 24/7.	**PROCESSES** Software delivery Professional services Support Project management Software lifecycle	**PRODUCTION PARTNERS** Software platform co	
CHANNEL PARTNERS Hardware providers Software consultants Other software co's Industry organization Trade shows		**BUSINESS MODEL** Offering includes software sold individually or as a suite and services for integration/ installation of software	**KNOWLEDGE/IP** Five software products Scripts for integration	**COMPETENCIES** Integration solutions .NET programming Industry platform Interoperability standards Healthcare experience	
	STAKEHOLDERS Patients Doctors Nurses Employees		**TANGIBLE ASSETS** Computers/servers Office furniture	**CULTURE** Can-do attitude Entrepreneurial Team spirit	
Revenue		Profits		Op Costs + Tangible + Intangible Capital Expenditures	
Reputation and Valuation					

Figure 1: Questionnaire Inventory

Stakeholders were asked to rate each of the IC elements on a scale from 1-5 as follows:

1. Worst
2. Below Average
3. Average
4. Above Average
5. Best

Stakeholders were given the names of comparable companies (these were also well known to them) in order to orient their judgment around what would be considered "average" in this company's market. It should be noted that in later refinements of this approach, the methodology shifted to asking about meeting stakeholder expectations (1-Unacceptable, 2-Does not meet expectations, 3-Meets expectations, 4-Exceeds expectations and 5-Excellent). This shift reflected a growing comfort among client companies with the validity of measuring themselves against stakeholder expectations (rather than measuring against their competitors as the "average" scale implies) such as those seen in on-line sites like Amazon, TripAdvisor and Glassdoor.

Stakeholder comments were also captured and recorded in combination with the ratings. Responses were typed by the consultant doing the interview in a web-based survey tool. Generic office software was used to perform the analysis, create graphs and build the final report.

The stakeholder sample was developed collaboratively with company management. It included a diverse, 360-degree sample:

- Internal management-level (6 people)
- Internal operations-level (9 people)
- External management-level (5 people)
- External management-level (6 people)

This sample represented roughly half of the company's total employees, most of the company's clients with large projects underway and represented 5% of the full license-paying client base.

Each stakeholder was interviewed for 30-60 minutes. The ratings were useful for getting specific feedback but equally important were the comments and observations that the stakeholders shared as they went along. The IC framework was helpful for teasing out feedback about the company. Detailed questions got the stakeholders thinking and they often offered suggestions for improvement and/or potential innovations.

Having a diverse sample was important for credibility of the findings. In the majority of the cases, all four stakeholder groups assigned similar ratings of IC elements. So this made it easy for users accept the validity of the rating. There were a few cases where there was disagreement among the stakeholders. Rather than undermine confidence in the numbers, these cases carried their own lessons, highlighting cases where further investigation was recommended. An example of this is discussed below.

3   Key challenges

There were three main challenges that arose over the course of the project:

Getting to the core IC elements – It took some iteration to refine the specific inventory of intangibles. This was a function of the fungible nature of the knowledge at the root of most intangibles. A capability of the company is often manifest in human capital competencies, structural capital processes and even strategic capital culture. An effort was made to avoid duplication of the same capabilities across all the forms of capital, classifying each in the category where it was most important or most obvious.

Making sense of all the data – Four IC categories, 12 resource subcategories, 66 questions and responses from four different stakeholder groups produces a lot of information. The solution was a series of graphs seen below. The key findings did come through clearly enabling the diagnostic to spark a number of productive improvements in the company.

Building a more permanent measurement system – The original intention of the project was to follow it up by creating a more traditional measurement system that could be used to track progress on a monthly basis. This proved to be more challenging as it was hard to find KPI's that gave as clear a read as the qualitative assessments.

4   Participant feedback

The data received a lot of respect from company managers because it represented a consensus of all the stakeholder groups that were important to the company's success. While there were a few surprises, much of the information made sense to the team. So, while there was value in the data itself, the main value appeared to come from a consistent, holistic view across all the functions of the company and from the clear calls for action that came out of the analysis.

5   Project outcomes

5.1   Assessment Findings

The summary findings of the assessment are illustrated in Figure 2. This summary shows graphically that two of the key issues blocking growth were the company's ability to leverage partnerships and lack of brand awareness. The good news was that the external market opportunity was very strong and the company's technology also received high markets. The technology score was especially encouraging as the company had built its software offerings from scratch over the previous ten years.

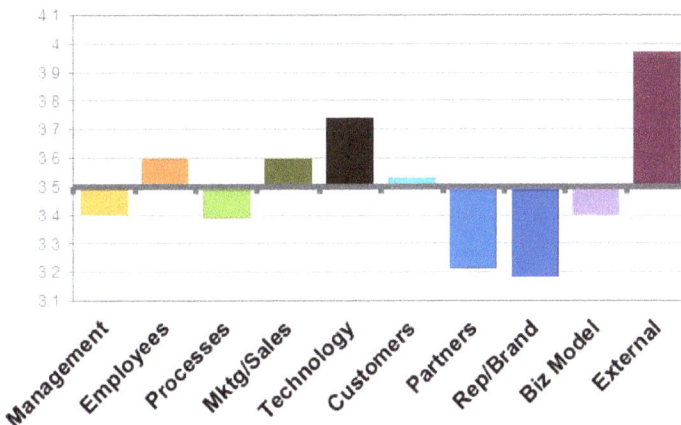

Figure 2: Summary of Findings

The full report included scores for individual questions and comments captured in the stakeholder interviews. The highest and lowest scores across all the questions are shown in Figure 3.

Key risks to current business	Key opportunities for the future
Brand consistency	Strong technology
Sales processes	Growing market
External partnership development	Project management offering
Project management processes	Co-innovation projects

Figure 3: Highest and Lowest Scores

These highlights were especially helpful to the management team as they grabbled with their stalled growth and desire to create a map to long-term value:

The opportunities were very good news for the team:

- Market – The growth prospects in the market were the highest rated item in the assessment. This told management that growth was possible, they just needed to find the right path.
- Technology – The company's software received very high marks. This was very encouraging to this relatively young company and gave them confidence to move forward more aggressively in the market.
- Co-innovation – The strength of its technologies meant more than the possibility of software sales; it also meant that the company had developed the confidence of its customers—and that the customers wanted the company to support them with higher-level services. This was basically an invitation to help solve the cutting-edge challenges faced by its customers and co-innovate future products.

The key risks made it clear why their sales were lagging despite the clear strengths listed above:

- Brand – Although those who knew the company thought highly of it, most potential customers still didn't really know the company. There needed to be more marketing outreach to support the brand.
- Sales processes – There were also weaknesses in the sales processes which was another limit on sales growth.
- External partnerships – The company's customers often have up to 50 different kinds of software in use on an on-going basis. This meant that learning to leverage relationships with other vendors was a valid strategy for growth. However, this company had not been successful with this type of relationship building.

5.2   Project Management Findings –

The project management is shown as both a risk and opportunity in Figure 3 and provided an especially interesting story. This was a rating where there were significant differences across stakeholder groups as seen in Figure 4. What was happening with this score? As the company had grown, the size of the implementations they were doing was also growing. Their strong culture and can-do attitude ensured that the customers were still satisfied. But the process of managing the projects was getting more chaotic.

- External managers who signed the contracts and had a big-picture exposure to the implementations knew that the software worked as expected and that they were satisfied with the results
- External operations staff who were in the middle of the implementations saw a few more of the glitches in the process
- Internal operations staff, also in the middle of the implementations, experienced the glitches and were honest with themselves about their weaknesses
- Internal management saw the big picture pattern: there were more and more crises. The crises were still getting resolved but management worried that the next crisis might be visible to the clients and harder to solve

Figure 4: Project management findings

This finding highlighted the clear risk that a large project could face serious delays and costly problems. Interestingly, however, the discussion of how to deal with this risk lead the company to realize that it created a revenue opportunity. If they were going to provide more explicit and professional project management, they would be able to charge for it.

5.3 Comments

Respondent comments also yielded fruitful feedback. An example of this was the theme that emerged around the opportunity for the company to offer high-level services in addition to their software. A few comments that illustrated this feedback included:

- *Co has throttled itself by not being more service focused. It has lost ground by not offering a fuller solution-service wrapper.*
- *Their products are easier to use, so maybe they don't sell as many professional services. Other companies probably sell more professional services because their products are harder to use.*
- *I worked for a software vendor for five years. I lost touch with my customers. I believe that being inside the customer's life helps us get to the pain points and solutions. Co could benefit from this through more professional services.*

These comments were challenging for the company to hear. They had worked hard to develop great software products that stood on their own. But the quality of this work had earned them the respect of their clients— who wanted the company to work with them on their leading edge problems. This came to be understood as an opportunity for getting paid to learn about the challenges that could become their next generation products through a high-end consulting offering.

5.4   Planning

The full final report was shared with the middle and top-level managers of the company. A summary report was shared with all employees as well as external stakeholders including those who had participated in the ratings.

The report was used as the starting point for the company's annual strategic planning process which was organized around five key questions that came out of the assessment about if/how the company should:

1. Move beyond its core market?
2. Become a more proactive partner to its clients?
3. Improve its project management capabilities?
4. Use external partnerships to fuel growth?
5. Develop new services/solutions?

All of these questions were a direct outcome of the IC assessment findings and were used to involve multiple levels of managers in developing plans to mitigate risks and leverage opportunities.

5.5   Execution

The strategic planning session and management meetings led to the implementation of a number of new initiatives over the following two years including:

- Reorganize sales group and improve sales processes
- Improve software R&D processes

- Improve project management processes
- Create new high-end services offering
- Create offering to charge for project management
- Launch a new corporate website
- Develop a business plan presentation (which included the assessment findings)
- Use the business plan to communicate with banks

These initiatives led to a number of strong outcomes:

- First bank line –The company incorporated the IC assessment into its business plan presentation. The data were presented in the financial section as a kind of alternative balance sheet, between the discussions of historical and projected financials as a presentation of "Current Capacity." Although the company had been turned down in the past, this business plan enabled them to get a bank line on very favorable terms.
- Revenue growth – After experiencing flat growth in the previous year, the company's revenues grew by 27% in the first year after completing the IC assessment and pursuing the described initiatives.
- Continued profitability – Process improvements ensured that the growth also led to continued strong levels of profitability.

It's important to be clear that the IC measurement did not, in itself, change the company's results. Rather, it provided information about intangible capital that, while important, had never been measured by this company in an objective way. The findings led to the initiatives that, collectively generated the strong results highlighted here.

5.6   Reporting and Measurement

The final phase of the project was aimed at creating a system of follow-on measures to support on-going operations and strategic management. This process went through several iterations using key performance indicators (KPI's) for the major teams and departments. This was the least successful of the initiatives in that the company still struggles with finding the right set of operating metrics to guide day-to-day management. As it turned out, KPI's do not provide the same kind or value of information as a stakeholder assessment.

6 Building on the initiative

6.1 At the company

The basic framework of the IC inventory and the business plan continue to be used by the company. The management team continues to refine its management metrics. They have not repeated the full-scale qualitative assessment process used in this project because it is an expensive under-taking to have individuals personally interviewed by consultants. They are, however, part of the beta test group for a lower-cost, on-line software version of stakeholder measurement of the company's core intangible capital. It is hoped that a platform for continuous feedback would help incorporate qualitative feedback side by side with KPI's on an on-going basis.

6.2 At the consulting company

The approach used in this project has been further refined and has led to a number of innovations and initiatives

- An open source intangible capital inventory worksheet that con-tinues to be refined based on market practice. The latest version of the worksheet adds natural capital in an effort to increase compatibility with integrated reporting projects.
- An interactive report using Tableau software to enable companies to review the data from projects such as this one in a more dy-namic fashion. The interactive report enables analysis by individ-ual questions, capital categories (human, relationship, etc), stake-holder groups and different groupings of stakeholder comments.
- A prototype of an on-line software platform that captures feed-back using a generic set of 20 intangible capital resources (four in

Mary Adams

each of five categories: strategic, structural, human, relationship and natural).

Beyond continuing to expand on these initiatives, there are interesting opportunities going forward for exploring the intersection between the intangible capital model and the integrated reporting model put forth by the International Integrated Reporting Council (IIRC).

Innovative Contribution to Organisational Knowledge Management Strategy: A Team Action Learning Initiative

Ghosia Ahmed[1], Gillian Ragsdell[1], Wendy Olphert[1], Mike Colechin[2]

[1] Loughborough University, Loughborough, United Kingdom
[2] The Energy Technologies Institute, Loughborough, United Kingdom

g.ahmed@lboro.ac.uk

Abstract

The paradoxical requirements of knowledge sharing and information security bring various knowledge management (KM) issues that affect both individuals' day-to-day work and the overall organisation's performance. This was the basis of a case study tackled by a team from Loughborough University.

The Energy Technologies Institute (ETI) is an organisation that combines knowledge and expertise from partnerships with academia, industry and the UK government, in order to deliver innovative low carbon solutions. Operating within a complex governance structure, the organisation works to meet the expectations of various stakeholders, comply with legal parameters of its membership model (to protect its unique knowledge and arising intellectual property), deliver innovative solutions many of which are of a competitive nature, and, disseminate this knowledge effectively and on time. Thus, the management of both, 'knowledge sharing' and 'information security', is an operational challenge for the ETI.

15

The aim of the KM initiative was to (i) understand the current knowledge sharing and information security practices at the ETI and (ii) identify ways of improving knowledge sharing within and beyond the organisation.

The KM initiative consisted of the development of a innovative and creative Action Learning (AL) approach through which ETI project teams combined their knowledge and experiences to identify their organisation's current knowledge sharing and information security practices and collectively devised practical solutions. Thus, through the combined effort of its project teams, the ETI was able to learn effectively and efficiently as an organisation about its challenges and the subsequent changes required, incorporate these in its KM strategy and initiate relevant changes to improve its KM. In addition to the value and benefits it has brought for the ETI, this innovative initiative has made methodological, theoretical and practical contributions to and received excellent feedback from international KM and AL communities.

1   The initiative and its specific objectives

Knowledge sharing is recognised as an essential activity for organisational success, hence organisations continuously aim to exploit existing knowledge, seek new ways to improve and increase knowledge sharing activities, as well as to identify and reduce possible knowledge sharing barriers. Similarly, protecting their valuable knowledge and intellectual property (IP) through information security measures is equally important for organisations. Information security measures aim to prevent the loss or leakage of an organisation's valuable information and manage the resulting cost of any loss. So, on the one hand knowledge sharing aims to encourage individuals to share knowledge with colleagues, organisational partners and suppliers, and on the other hand, information security initiatives aim to apply controls and restrictions to the knowledge that can be shared and how it is shared.

The intrinsically paradoxical requirements of knowledge sharing and information security (see Figure 1) bring various challenges that affect both individuals' day-to-day work and the overall organisation's performance. These challenges formed the basis of a case study tackled by a team from Loughborough University.

Figure 1: The conflict of interest between knowledge sharing and information security

The case study was carried out with the Energy Technologies Institute (ETI) – a UK-based organisation that is a public-private partnership set-up by the UK government and global energy and engineering companies - BP, Caterpillar, EDF Energy, Rolls-Royce and Shell. By combining the knowledge and expertise from partnerships with academia, industry and the UK government, the ETI researches, develops and delivers innovation in low carbon energy solutions that will help the UK address its long term emissions reductions targets. Operating within a complex governance structure, the ETI works to meet the expectations of various stakeholders, comply with legal parameters of its membership model (to protect its unique knowledge and arising IP), deliver innovative solutions (many of which are of a competitive nature) and, disseminate this knowledge effectively and on time. Thus, the management of both, 'knowledge sharing' and 'information security', is an operational challenge for the ETI.

1.1 Objectives of the Knowledge Management initiative

In order to identify ways in which the ETI can improve its knowledge sharing by effectively managing the relationship between its knowledge sharing and information security practices, understanding the current state of the two practices was vital. Therefore, the objectives of the KM initiative were to:

i. understand the current knowledge sharing and information security practices at the ETI, and,
ii. identify ways of improving knowledge sharing within and beyond the organisation.

Using an Action Learning (AL) approach, central to the KM initiative design was the input from employees. The employees involved in the initiative not only participated by sharing their knowledge and experiences of the two practices and identifying the current issues, but they also became more empowered as teams to develop appropriate solutions that informed the organisation's KM strategy and initiated effective organisational change.

This case history discusses the infrastructure of the KM initiative and how an innovative and successful team AL approach was developed (section 2), the challenges that were encountered, how they developed and were overcome (section 3), as well as, how the initiative was received by the users or participants (section 4). How the efficiency and effectiveness outcomes were achieved and how they were measured (section 5) will also be discussed, followed by how the initiative was taken forward and what its contribution to the KM and AL communities is (section 6).

2 The infrastructure required to launch the initiative

2.1 Role of people

Knowledge sharing is an activity that happens intentionally and voluntarily, and much of it in an organisation occurs between *individuals*. Equally, although information security measures are typically implemented and governed by dedicated individuals or teams in the organisation (such as IT), their impact in practice can only really be assessed through understanding the employees' day-to-day experiences of information security.

By taking into account the integral role of employees in the current practices, it was recognised that the KM initiative would need to be designed with the knowledge and experiences of the employees at its core. To elicit individual's knowledge and experiences and develop a snapshot of the knowledge sharing and information security practices, any qualitative data collection method, such as one-to-one interviews, questionnaires or focus groups, would have been sufficient. However, the aim of this initiative was more than understanding the current practices; the intention was to develop ways of improving practice, which would subsequently lead to improved organisational effectiveness and efficiency. Therefore, it was critical that the employees were engaged and become an active part of the initiative that would drive organisational change. With that in mind, a creative and novel AL approach was developed.

2.2 Approach and steps used to launch the initiative

"The end of learning is action, not knowledge" -Peter Honey

AL is a process of reflection and learning to address and solve real organisation problems. The AL environment is specifically designed to be conducive to reflection, openness, knowledge sharing and learning. Additional to the learning that is generated by and for the employees involved in AL, the process can also facilitate organisational learning and be a powerful tool for transforming organisation culture, increasing learning capacity and empowering employees.

In conventional AL, a set of individuals are brought together for the purpose of AL, as opposed to using an intact team e.g. a departmental team or project team because of the additional complexities and group dynamics of an intact team such as relationships, hierarchy and the challenges of sticking to the AL principles e.g. confidentiality. However, for this initiative a novel and creative AL approach was developed where intact project teams at the ETI were specifically selected for participation in the AL sessions. The relationship between knowledge sharing and information security becomes even more important to explore in project environments as both practices are equally important to ensure that a novel product or service is achieved from the project (through the collective knowledge sharing of the team), yet it should give the organisation advantage over its competitors by protecting the knowledge which leads to that product or service being generated.

The KM initiative consisted of a cyclic AL approach with three project teams at the ETI.

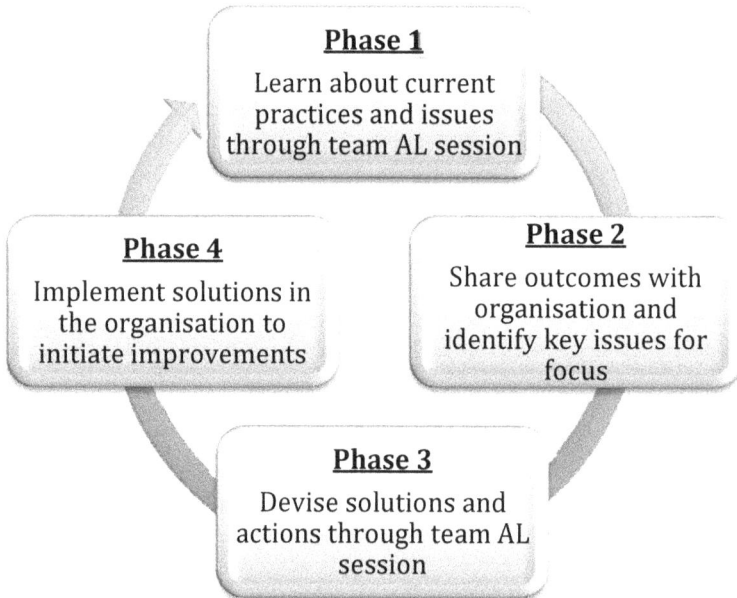

Figure 2: Design of the KM initiative

Phase 1
The aim of Phase 1 was to learn about the current knowledge sharing and information security practices. Three team AL sessions were set-up (with a duration of three hours each), all consisting of the following discussion themes.

- Theme 1: Knowledge sharing (i.e. strengths and weaknesses, level of awareness and the challenges).
- Theme 2: The organisational culture (i.e. what motivates people culturally to share knowledge and the role of management in supporting and nurturing knowledge sharing).
- Theme 3: Information security (i.e. strengths and weaknesses, level of awareness and the challenges).

Each theme consisted of a set of questions, encouraging participants to reflect on and share relevant experiences. For example, one of the questions in Theme 1 was *'What do you think the strengths and weaknesses are of knowledge sharing externally for the ETI?'*. By sharing their knowledge and experiences, the team engaged in deep discussions and reflection, and collectively developed a hierarchy of the key strengths and weaknesses of the ETI's knowledge sharing and information security practices.

Participants were also asked to complete a brief questionnaire by rating the effectiveness of various aspects of knowledge sharing and information security at the ETI.

Phase 2
Phase 2 of the initiative consisted of the analysis of the findings from Phase 1, a summary report for the ETI and a meeting with the ETI to share the findings and progress. Next, based on the Phase 1 findings, the second set of AL workshops were designed.

Phase 3
Phase 3 consisted of the second set of AL sessions (duration of three hours each) with the three project teams. During each session, the team's respective findings from Phase 1 were shared, focusing particularly on the

21

issues identified, which led to deeper discussions and the development of appropriate actions and solutions to help the ETI overcome these issues and improve its knowledge sharing.

Phase 4
In Phase 4, the outcomes of Phase 3 were analysed and the actions and solutions that the teams devised were shared with the ETI. The actions and solutions were then mapped against the existing KM activities to identify where they would be best aligned. Engagement took place with the project managers from each of the participating teams to help initiate the implementation of the KM initiative.

2.3   Role of technology

Since the initiative's purpose was to identify current knowledge sharing and information security problems and improve knowledge sharing throughout and beyond the organisation, the focus was on the social dimensions (such as the employees' knowledge, experiences and organisational processes), rather than technological dimensions. However, technology does play an important role in both knowledge sharing and information security, and therefore a number of technology related areas were specifically explored under each of the three themes discussed in section 2.2 (e.g. systems, electronic sharing tools and technical access controls).

3   The challenges that were encountered, how they developed and how they were overcome

Although the KM initiative was overall successful, a number of challenges were faced along the way that can be expected from an initiative that intends to drive organisational level change.

During Phase 1, a major challenge was obtaining buy-in from the three participating teams. During the session, some individuals questioned whether there was value for them in participating, what significance their involvement held and how they would benefit from it. This challenge was overcome by explaining the integral role of the participants in the initiative and how their collective reflection, knowledge and experience sharing would enable the ETI to learn about its current practices and the associated issues. Further, it was also explained that the findings from this phase of the initiative (in particular the problems identified) would inform the subsequent phases and the team would use this learning and have the authority to develop suitable actions and solutions.

Another challenge faced during the first phase of the initiative was to get the participants in the project teams to focus on their experiences of the current practices *'as they are'*, as opposed to how they *'should be'* (in theory). Thus, the participants had to be regularly reminded of this throughout the sessions.

During the second session (Phase 3) the teams were reminded of the outcomes of the first session and the issues they identified, and were asked to devise appropriate solutions and actions. It was challenging to shift the team's mindset from focusing on the problems to developing solutions. Some resistance was experienced from some of the participants in taking ownership of the solutions and actions they were devising. However, this was overcome once it was clarified that the solutions and actions being developed were not the sole responsibility of the team to implement and drive, but more so for them to champion the organisational level changes that will occur. Once the teams understood the value of the initiative and their role in driving organisational change, they became proactively engaged in developing the solutions and actions and took responsibility for championing the subsequent changes.

A logistical challenge faced was finding a suitable timeslot to set-up each of the sessions due to the busy schedules of the teams. After experiencing some difficulty with this in Phase 1, the subsequent sessions were planned and set-up well in advance.

4 How the initiative was received by the users or participants

For the KM initiative, three project teams were invited to voluntarily participate and each team responded positively. At the start, each participant was informed about the process of the initiative and what will be required from him or her in the form of participation, following which a consent form was completed. The participants were also briefed and assured of anonymity of their participation which helped to develop confidence and enabled them to participate without hesitation.

As discussed in section 3 earlier, during the initial stage of the initiative, buy-in from all of the participants was challenging and required further explanation of the aims and benefits. Once this was clear, the participants engaged enthusiastically and shared their knowledge, experiences and problems openly and honestly.

Further, in the second session (in Phase 3), despite the initial struggle, the participants in each of three project teams acted as a community and collectively devised solutions to the ETI's knowledge sharing and information security problems. The approach each of the teams took to devise the solutions and take ownership of championing the actions strongly suggested that the participants felt a sense of empowerment and responsibility in improving the organisation's practices through the KM initiative.

5 The outcomes that were achieved and how they were measured and evaluated

The KM initiative enabled the ETI to learn about its current knowledge sharing and information security practices, their associated strengths and weaknesses, and the nature of the relationship between the two conflicting practices. More importantly, the ETI learned about the impact of information security measures on knowledge sharing. Being too cautious and overprotective of its knowledge and IP had previously created knowledge sharing barriers that affected day-to-day activities of employees, resulted in missed opportunities for timely exploitation of project outcomes and consequently impacted the organisation's performance as a knowledge generating and disseminating organisation whose outputs are knowledge driven. Becoming aware of the issues that employees experience and receiving proposed solutions by those employees, provided the ETI with a distinctive and enriched view of where it was at that stage and which changes needed to be initiated to improve the efficiency and effectiveness of its KM.

The effectiveness and efficiency of the KM initiative were evaluated through the outputs achieved. Through the initiative, the ETI generated individual, team and organisational level learning as well as a new capacity to initiate organisational change through the engagement, trust and empowerment of its employees. Thus, the KM initiative has been important for initiating thoughtful and inclusive change. The learning and solutions developed throughout the KM initiative were incorporated in the ETI's KM strategy and aligned with relevant activities to improve knowledge sharing within and beyond the organisation.

6 Plans to further develop the initiative

The KM initiative was a part of a PhD research in collaboration with the ETI. The initiative has not only been fruitful for the ETI in initiating improvements to achieve more efficiency and effectiveness in its KM activities, but has also had international impact and brought methodological, theoretical and practical benefits for the KM and AL communities.

For the KM arena, this initiative has introduced a fresh and powerful methodological approach underpinned by AL that can drive effective organisational change. Very often, the focus of KM initiatives is on technological interventions or solutions, despite the employees, practices and processes playing an integral role in an organisation's KM. In terms of the practical benefits, through this initiative, it is evident that by focusing on and empowering employees, an organisation can learn about its specific KM related practices, identify the strengths and weaknesses and develop informed solutions. Further, the involvement of employees throughout the initiative and their buy-in strengthens the organisation's capability and forms a strong foundation from which to implement KM changes and improves the chances of their success. The methodology of this initiative was shared in the International Conference on Intellectual Capital and Knowledge Management (ICICKM 2014) in Sydney where it received considerable positive feedback and was awarded the prize for 'Best PhD paper and presentation'.

The AL community has received this KM initiative extremely favorably. The case study was shared in the Action Learning and Action Research Association (ALARA) conference Australia in November 2014 and also in a workshop run by the Action Learning for Facilitators (ALF) network in London in March 2015. Both audiences acknowledged the novelty of the approach and praised the innovative theoretical and practical application of AL at the team level to address and improve organisational practices. It was recognised that the team-based approach has the potential to change mindsets in the AL community about the ways and settings in which AL can be used. Subsequently, the ALF network has invited further contribution and enlightenment on this KM initiative in a workshop in December 2015.

Knowledge Repository: Ipea´s Knowledge Repository

Fábio Ferreira Batista, Veruska da Silva Costa

Instituto de Pesquisa Econômica Aplicada - Ipea, Brasília, Brazil
fabio.batista@ipea.gov.br

Abstract

The Institute for Applied Economic Research, or Instituto de Pesquisa Econômica Aplicada (Ipea), as it is known in Brazil, is a public foundation linked to the Brazilian Presidency. Its research activities aid the government in planning and implementing public policies.

Ipea´s Knowledge Repository (RCIpea) is a very useful KM initiative that allows users inside and outside the organization to access the institute's intellectual capital. The repository is an online portal designed to preserve and manage the institute's organizational memory. RCIpea contains more than documents (a document management system), data (database), or records (a record management system). It also contains valuable knowledge comprised of the combination of the organization's tacit and explicit knowledge based on Ipea's researchers' unique experiences in terms of conducting social studies research.

Researchers' tacit knowledge has been stored in the repository through videos where researchers share their own lessons learned and best practices.

The RCIpea allowed the institute to make explicit part of the researchers' tacit knowledge. Today, the institute's tacit and explicit knowledge are organized and stored in a structured way. Moreover, this knowledge can now be disseminated using patterns of international interoperability, allowing internal and external access to Ipea's knowledgebase.

The implementation of RCIpea shows that it is possible to implement a KM framework, a KM method, and a KM practice in an integrated way. The KM Framework for the Brazilian Public Administration designed by Fábio Ferreira Batista is the foundational theory, developed through a literature review covering KM frameworks in the public sector (Batista, 2012). Following this decision, a KM Plan was draft based on an implementation method for that purpose. The main focus was the implementation of a repository to eliminate knowledge gaps and to improve organizational performance.

1 Introduction

The Institute for Applied Economic Research (Ipea) sees Knowledge Management as an integrated method to create, share, and apply knowledge to improve organizational performance. In other words, KM is not an end in itself. Its implementation should bring results for the Institute's employees and managers, as well as to Brazilian citizens by allowing Ipea, a public sector organization, to fulfill its mission.

In 2012, Ipea decided to adopt a KM Framework designed specifically for the Brazilian public sector (Batista, 2012).

The first KM framework component: the importance of KM strategy alignment with the organization's strategic planning to ensure KM initiatives will contribute toward the fulfillment of the organization's strategic objectives. Public sector organizations should answer the following questions, in this order: First: what is our mission? Second: how are we going to achieve our vision, in terms of the kind of organization we want to be ten, fifteen, or twenty years from now? Third: what core knowledge or core competencies do our employees and managers require to achieve our strategic objectives and goals. Only after asking these questions should organizations ask how knowledge should be managed to fulfill its mission and reach its vision. Therefore, KM initiatives should help organizations achieve its strategic objectives in order to be considered an important approach.

KM success factors or enablers are the second framework component, which include leadership, technology, people, and processes.

Leadership in a successful KM implementation effort ensures that KM projects are aligned with organizational strategic goals and that these will improve performance, and provides the necessary resources (financial, technological, and human).

Technology is also an important enabler. Information technology and communication tools help organizations better manage knowledge processes (knowledge identification, creation, storage, sharing, and application).

People play the most important role in KM implementation, as they are responsible for all knowledge processes. Moreover, they own the organization's most valuable intangible asset: tacit knowledge. Therefore, KM initiatives should focus on individual learning to improve employee performance, thereby improving team and organizational performance.

Finally, processes play an essential role in KM because the way organizations manage knowledge in managing processes is a decisive factor for performance improvement.

The third framework component is the KM process. There are five essential activities in the KM process to effectively manage knowledge to reach the organization's objectives: identification, creation, storage, sharing, and application of knowledge. These activities should be an essential part of project and process management. In 2009, Ipea adopted the KM operational cycle shown in Figure 1, where knowledge is managed as a regular activity in project and process management.

The KDCA Cycle has four stages. The KM plan is designed in the first stage: **Knowledge (K)**. Employees are trained, a KM plan is implemented, and data and information are collected in the second stage, **DO (D)**. The third stage, **CHECK   (C)**, is the moment to check if the quality goals were achieved and if the KM plan was implemented as planned. Finally, if the goal was not met or there were mistakes during the KM implementation process activities (knowledge identification, creation, storage, sharing, and application) should be fixed during the fourth stage, **ACT (A)**. If it was, then the knowledge should be stored in the Knowledge Repository to later re-use.

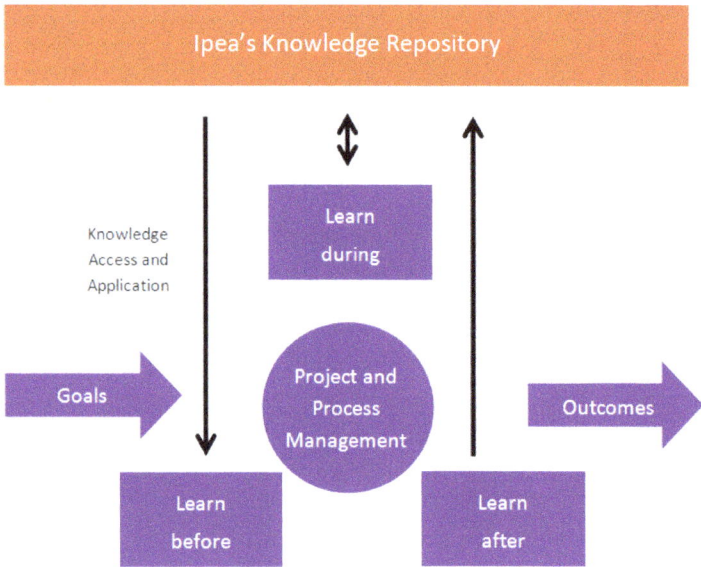

Source: Adapted from APO, 2009.

Figure 1 – Ipea's KM Operational Cycle

The KM outcomes comprise the fifth framework component. KM implementation should result in both intermediate and final outcomes. The intermediate results include learning and innovation, and thus enhance individual, team, organizational, and social capacity to identify, create, store, share, and apply knowledge. Intermediate outcomes should enable organizations to reach the final outcomes: enhanced efficiency, higher quality and effectiveness, and an improved capacity to fulfill the constitutional principles of Brazilian public administration (legality, impersonality, morality, and transparency) and promoting development.

Stakeholders are the final KM framework component, and include citizens and society overall. All public sector organizations should manage knowledge about citizens to fulfill their mission and meet society's needs and expectations about the quality of public services.

2 Designing a Successful KM Strategy and Plan

In 2012, Ipea designed their KM strategy and plan in seven steps, based on Ipea's KM Framework described in the introduction. The first step is to identify a major knowledge problem. In the previous year, a KM team assessed Ipea's information and knowledge needs and found that the leadership as well as senior and junior researchers complained about the difficulty in getting the right information and knowledge to the right people at the right time within the organization. Although all papers, reports, and books were stored in the organization's portal, researchers reported that they were not easy to find. Therefore, it was clear to the KM team that solving the problem required some kind of knowledgebase as the portal was not a suitable place to store information and knowledge that researchers need in their daily tasks.

The second stage was to establish a KM vision: "Researchers can access key explicit and tacit knowledge to learn from before implementing research projects, that is, accessing and applying existing knowledge, to learn during the project and continuously access that knowledge, and to learn after, either validating or renewing the knowledge stored in the organization, to improve Ipea's performance." This vision is aligned with Ipea's KM Operational Cycle shown in Figure 1.

Based on this vision, the team established the KM goal in the third: "To make available, both internally and externally, and with fast access, key explicit and tacit knowledge produced by Ipea's researchers, consultants, and visiting scholars." In the fourth stage, the team defined the KM Strategy: "To identify, organize, store, and disseminate for quick access, use, and reuse, key explicit and tacit knowledge produced internally to improve Ipea's performance."

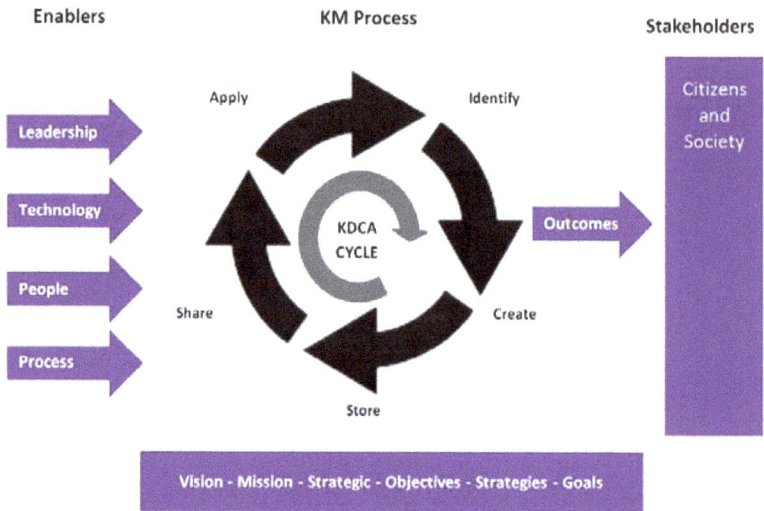

Source: Batista, (2012).

Figure 2: KM Framework for the Brazilian Public Administration

Metrics were established in the fifth step to monitor KM's strategy results: 1) Percentage of key tacit and explicit knowledge identified, organized, stored, and disseminated internally and externally; 2) Researchers' satisfaction with access to information and knowledge needed to implement projects; 3) Researchers' satisfaction with research project outcomes as a result of the KM initiative. The sixth step was to design and implement a KM Plan for Ipea's KM Repository of the key tacit and explicit knowledge the organization produces. Finally, the seventh step was to continually monitor and assess the KM plan to determine if the KM goal is being achieved.

3   Introduction to the initiative and its specific objectives

Ipea's knowledge repository is recognized as a KM practice in the organization. From its initial implementation in 2012, its main goal was to solve a knowledge problem detected in a KM assessment completed in 2011. The knowledge produced by Ipea's researchers was not captured, represented, organized, and stored in a way that allows quick access and use by both the researchers and outside stakeholders (government officials and public employees, citizens, private companies, unions, research institutes, universities, and so on).

For research institutions, repositories are now considered a KM practice and a strategic tool to enhance visibility. Repositories allow knowledge dissemination in scientific and technical communities (Costa and Leite, 2006).

The repository's specific objectives were: to allow users inside and outside the organization to access the institute's intellectual capital; to preserve and manage the institute's organizational memory; to contain more than documents (a document management system), data (database), or records (a record management system) but also the valuable knowledge comprised of the combination of the organization's tacit and explicit knowledge based on Ipea's researchers' unique experiences in terms of conducting social studies research; to store researchers' tacit knowledge through videos where researchers share their own lessons learned and best practices; to make explicit part of the researchers' tacit knowledge; to organize and store in a structured way the institute's tacit and explicit knowledge; and to disseminate knowledge using patterns of international interoperability, allowing internal and external access to Ipea's knowledgebase.

Ipea's repository has several features: search tools; search by topic; communities and collections; browse by author, subject, and date; browse by type; and storytelling videos, as shown in Figures 3 - 7.

Fábio Ferreira Batista, Veruska da Silva Costa

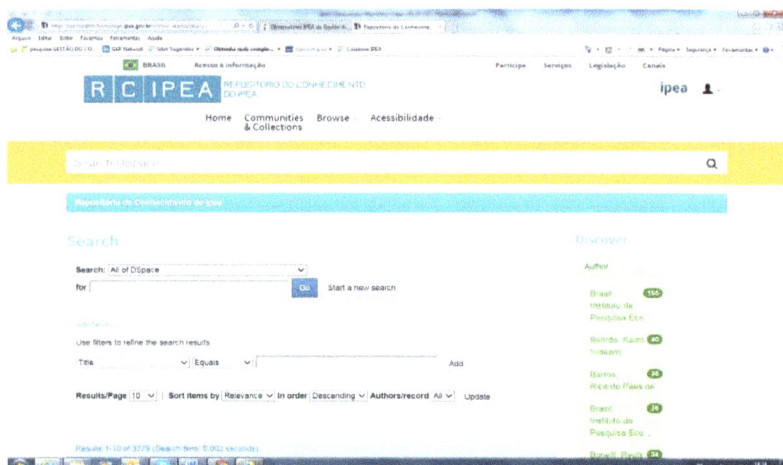

Source: http://repositorio.ipea.gov.br/

Figure 3: Search tool

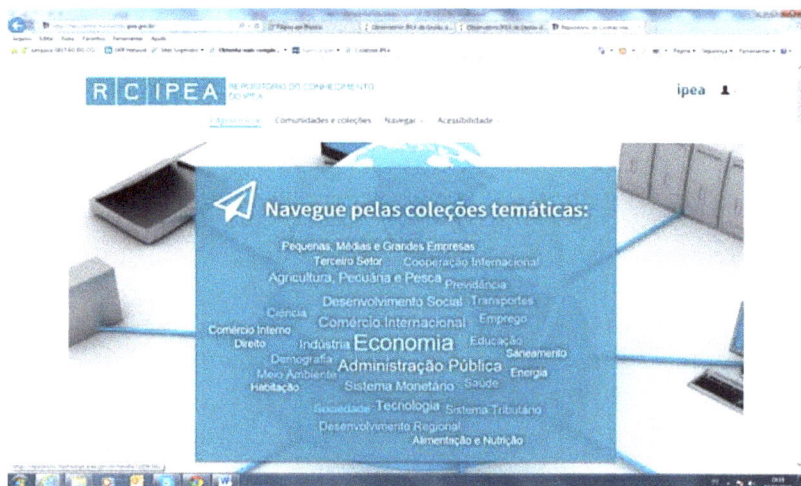

Source: http://repositorio.ipea.gov.br/

Figure 4: Search by topic

34

Fábio Ferreira Batista, Veruska da Silva Costa

- **Communities and collections**: 1) public administration, government, and state; 2) agriculture, livestock, and fishery; 3) food and
  nutrition; 4) science, research, methodology, and data analysis; 5)
  international trade; 6) domestic trade; 7) international cooperation and international relations; 8) demography and population;
  9) regional development; 10) social development; 11) law and leg-
  islation; 12) economy and economic development; 13) education;
  14) employment and labor; 15) energy; 16) housing; 17) industry;
  18) environment and natural resources; 19) small, medium, and
  large companies; 20) social security; 21) sanitation; 22) health; 23)
  monetary system, finance, and banking; 24) tax system; 25) society, social participation, and social control; 26) technology, innovation, information, and knowledge; 27) third sector, services, and
  tourism; and 28) transportation.

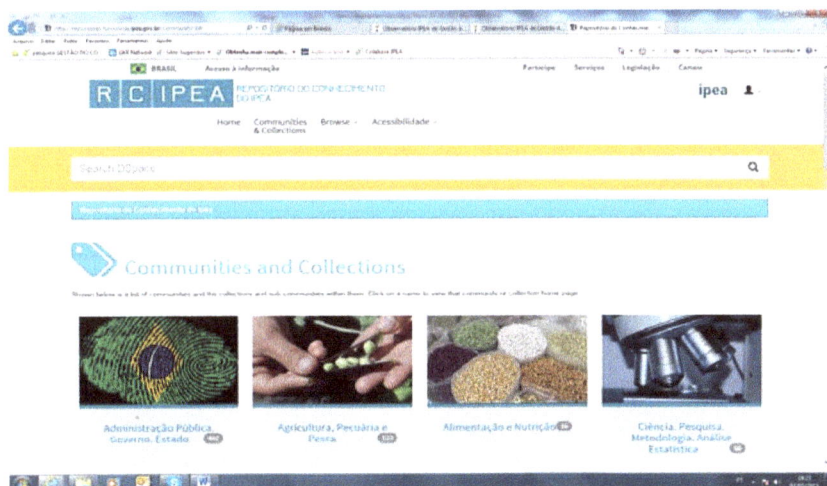

Source: http://repositorio.ipea.gov.br/

Figure 5: Communities and collections

35

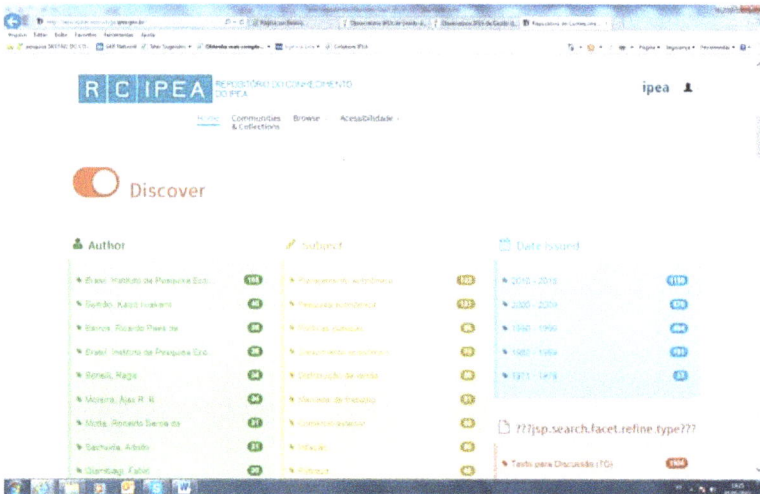

Source: http://repositorio.ipea.gov.br/
Figure 6 – Browse by author, subject, and date

Storytelling videos, in which Ipea's researchers share lessons learned during research projects and describe the impact of Ipea's papers on public policy formation and implementation, are important objects in the repository as they preserve organizational memory. The repository also includes videos with Ipea's managers, wherein they share lessons learned, and best practices in process management.

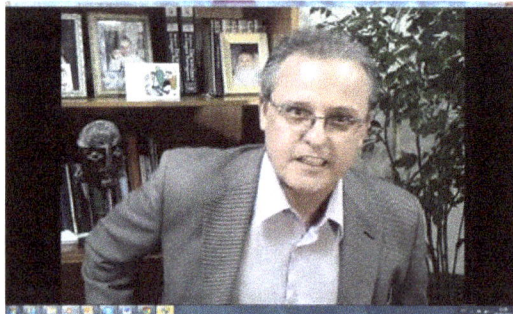

Source:http://repositorio.ipea.gov.br/
Figure 8 – Storytelling videos

3.1   The infrastructure required to launch the initiative

The Knowledge Repository was implemented by a multidisciplinary team from diverse areas including: the KM Unit, Project Management Office, Library Division, Information Technology (IT) Department, Communication Division, and Research Departments. The repository's implementation effort was led by the KM team and sponsored by the head of the Institutional Development Department, which assured financial resources in addition to the personnel and consultants required to successfully implement the project.

The participation of a multidisciplinary team in the repository design and implementation provided the necessary support, collaboration, and involvement of Ipea's key stakeholders (Batista and Costa, 2013).

The repository implementation was also made possible by the work of a team of experts with extensive expertise in the following issues: Dspace software, information architecture, domain study, metadata definition (Dublin Core), repository flows, access policy and copyrights, metadata filling, software installation and customization, and visual identity, among others.

The chosen software, Dspace, was developed by the Massachusetts Institute of Technology (MIT) and the company Hewlett-Packard (HP).

Dspace was chosen because it: 1) has the largest community of users and developers worldwide; 2) is free and open source software; 3) is completely customizable to fit Ipea's needs; and 4) is used by educational, government, private, and commercial institutions worldwide, including: Harvard University, MIT, Yale University, Princeton University, Johns Hopkins University, George Washington University, the University of Cambridge, Georgetown University, São Paulo University (Brazil), and Brasilia University (Brazil), among others; 5) can be installed out of the box; and 6) can manage and preserve all types of digital content.

The minimum necessary requirements were employed: the Linux Operational System, Java JDK 1.7 +, Maven 3+, Tomcat 7+, Ant 1.7+, and PostgreSQL 9.x_. Moreover, the project used the following initial infrastructure: four Entral Processing Units, four GB of RAM memory, and 500 GB of disk space.

3.2 The challenges that were encountered, how they developed and how they were overcome

There were challenges encountered related to technology, people, and processes. Ipea's IT department was not familiar with the Dspace software, a critical problem because IT support is essential for the repository's successful implementation. To overcome this obstacle, an outside expert was hired to both provide assistance in the project implementation and share knowledge with the IT team.

Another challenge was the fact that the Library Division's employees were not familiar with the repository's implementation. Although all were highly experienced in librarian services, none were familiar with knowledge repositories. This was overcome by hiring a repository expert to join the KM team to provide guidelines and training to the Library Division's personnel and all employees involved in the project. Another challenge was to clarify the roles for all areas involved in the repository's implementation and management. This was accomplished by issuing of an ordinance signed by Ipea's president with the description of all tasks to be performed by every stakeholder.

3.3 How the initiative was received by the users and participants

The KM initiative was well received by Ipea's researchers because it eventually helped them in their daily research activities by improving knowledge access and use. External stakeholders also welcomed the KM practice for the same reasons. However, Library Division's team, one of the most important participants of the KM initiative, presented some resistance in the beginning because they saw the KM Unit initiative as a threat since they did not have a leading role in its implementation and management. The leadership commitment to the project and efforts by the KM Unit team demonstrated the important role the Library Division was going to play in the repository's implementation and management.

3.4   The outcomes that were achieved and how they were measured and evaluated

This case history collected the following data covering the main indicators Ipea used to measure and evaluate the Knowledge Repository, covering the period from January 2012 to April 2015:

- Total items published: 2.775;
- Number of storytelling videos: 10;
- Percentage of Ipea's most important publication, "Text for Discussion," published in the repository: 2.056 (100%);
- Percentage of the most important series of books published by Ipea ("Brazil in Development" and "Brazil: The State of the Union") added to the repository: 100%;
- Number of countries that accessed the repository: 120;
- Number of cities that accessed the repository: 2.245;
- Number of continents that accessed the repository: 6;

From January 2013 to December 2014, the following results were found:

- Viewed items: 842.868;
- Viewed collections: 260.528;
- Users' Logins: 4.175;
- Number of searches: 44.256

4   Plans to further develop the initiative

The following projects and activities are planned for implementation in the next three years to further develop the repository:

- **Federation of Repositories for Development.** This KM initiative will gather the intellectual production of several Brazilian research organizations dedicated to development issues. Ipea's repository will be the first to join the Federation, making available its OAI-PMH Interface;
- **Lessons Learned System.** The tacit knowledge of Ipea's experts about lessons learned in research projects will be captured in workshops, and organized and stored in the repository for internal and external dissemination;
- **Best Practice System.** The tacit knowledge of best research practices and methods used by Ipea's researchers will be captured in workshops, and organized and stored accordingly.
- **Storytelling in the Repository.** Ipea will continue to capture its researchers' tacit knowledge by recording their stories and including these in the Knowledge repository.
- **User satisfaction survey.** A satisfaction survey will be conducted in September 2015 to understand Ipea's researchers' level of satisfaction with the knowledge repository and to gather employees' opinions about how to improve the KM initiative.
- **Ipea's Expert Yellow Pages linked to the Knowledge Repository.** A Yellow Pages directory linked to the repository's objects will be implemented using metadata.

Ipea's knowledge repository has helped the organization reach the KM goal established in 2012. Researcher's tacit and explicit knowledge have been stored, little by little, in the repository and their fast access is now possible for both internal and external stakeholders. The leadership and the KM team are aware that Ipea is on the right track to build a comprehensive knowledge base, including all or nearly all of the organization's essential knowledge. However, it is also clear that this is just the beginning of a continuous process.

Fábio Ferreira Batista, Veruska da Silva Costa

References

APO. (2009) Knowledge management: facilitator's Guide. Disponível em: http://www.apo-tokyo.org/00e-books/IS-39_APO-KM-FG.htm. Acessado em: May 7, 2015.

Batista, F. F. (2012). Modelo de Gestão do Conhecimento para a Administração Pública Brasileira. Como implementar a Gestão do Conhecimento para produzir resultados em benefício do cidadão. Brasília: Ipea.

Batista, F. F.; Costa (2013), V. S. Alinhando o modelo, o método de implementação e a prática de gestão do conhecimento (GC): O caso do Repositório do Conhecimento do Instituto de Pesquisa Econômica Aplicada (RClpea). Revista do Serviço Público, v. 64, n.1, p. 59-76, jan./mar.

Costa, S. M. S; Leite, F. C. L. (2006). Repositórios institucionais como ferramentas de gestão do conhecimento científico no ambiente acadêmico. **Perspect. ciênc. inf.**, Belo Horizonte, v.11 n.2, p. 206 -219, mai./ago. Disponível em: http://www.scielo.br/pdf/%0D/pci/v11n2/v11n2a05.pdf . Acesso em: February 22, 2013.

Fábio Ferreira Batista, Veruska da Silva Costa

Mass Collaborative Knowledge Processing on the Semantic Web

Chaolemen Borjigen
Renmin University of China
chaolemen@ruc.edu.cn

Abstract

We are entering into a new era of mass collaboration and there are significant changes in awareness of knowledge protection, environments of knowledge sharing, drivers of knowledge processing, and participation of knowledge agents. However, the study of knowledge processing has not been kept up with these new trends. This project conducted an in-depth study of knowledge processing on the semantic web utilizing OMT (Object Modeling Technology) methodology from a mass collaboration perspective and proposed its object model, functional model and agent interaction model. Theoretical foundations for the study are Semantic Web, Web2.0, Hall for Workshop of Meta-synthetic Engineering and Knowledge Ecology. Furthermore, the implementation framework and operational mechanism are described in order to meet the new challenges and to guide the application of the models. This study will be of great significance for promoting knowledge sharing, building open knowledge ecosystem, and resolving conflicts between size and formalization of data in the semantic knowledge base.

1 Introduction to the initiative and its specific objectives

We are entering into a new era of mass collaboration, and there are significant changes in awareness of knowledge protection, environments of knowledge sharing, drivers of knowledge processing, and participation of intelligent agents. However, existing knowledge management studies fail to meet these new challenges. This initiative aims to reveal the underlying principles of knowledge processing in a new era of mass collaboration and provide an integrated guideline for organizational knowledge management based on identifying the gaps between the existing knowledge management theories and emerging knowledge initiatives such as Web2.0, Pro-

43

Am, Crowd Source, as well as Open Innovation. **This initiative for the first time proposes a novel knowledge management paradigm called Mass Collaborative Knowledge Management (Table1) and provides its main principles, basic models, reference frameworks, and typical applications.**

1. It identifies the gaps between emerging practices and existing knowledge management theories.
2. It embraces the long tails into the scope of organizational knowledge management and extends the scope of prevailing knowledge management studies.
3. It turns to Pro-Ams instead of professionals and reduces the cost and risk in organizational knowledge management that depends mainly on professionals.
4. It highlights the advantages of opening organizational internal knowledge and transforms the core beliefs in conventional knowledge management.
5. It classifies organizational knowledge into two types (domain knowledge and non-domain knowledge) and provides different managing policies, respectively (Table2).

Table 1. Comparisons between the existing KM and Mass Collaborative KM

	The existing KM	Mass Collaborative KM
Hypothesis	All valuable knowledge comes from internal key staff at small heads of organizational knowledge chains	Most of valuable knowledge could be obtained from Pro-Ams at the long tails of organizational knowledge chains
Purpose	To create, capture, codify or share knowledge mainly by internal staff located at small heads of organizational knowledge chains	To produce knowledge emergence by fostering candidate staff at the long tails of organizational knowledge chains and addressing knowledge gaps between small heads and long tails
Perspective	Small head side	Long tail side
Scope	Limited in small heads of organizational knowledge chains: key staff's key knowledge	Extended to the scope of knowledge management to the long tails of the knowledge chains
Driver	Simplified ,performance evaluation	Diversified, personal interests, social recognition, competitive threat

Stand point	Professionals centered	Pro –Ams centered
Knowledge policy	Closed strictly	Open properly
Theoretical foundation	Self-organization and Complex Adaptive System (CAS) Theory	Web 2.0, Knowledge Ecology , Complexity Theory , Hall for Workshop of Meta-synthetic Engineering , Linked Data ,and Semantic Web
Enabler	Organizational learning	Mass collaboration
Approach	Man-man collaboration	Human-machine collaboration
Knowledge Classification	Individual, team, or organizational level knowledge	Domain knowledge and non-domain knowledge
Technologies	Traditional knowledge technologies	Semantic Web technologies

Introducing Mass Collaborative Knowledge Management into organizational knowledge management will not only promote the organizational knowledge sharing, but also help an organization build an open knowledge ecosystem. This is the first initiative to introduce a new direction of knowledge management studies, which guides an organization to build an open knowledge ecosystem by implementing collaborations between the long tails of its knowledge chains as well as taking advantages of the complementary advantages of man and machines in knowledge processing.

Table 2. Knowledge in the Semantic Web based Knowledge processing

	Domain knowledge	Non-domain knowledge
Definition	Basic knowledge in certain domains , such as terms, perspectives, principles, models, rules, technologies, and tools	One-off knowledge such as decision, fact, process
Features	Stable General Reusable Fundamental	Dynamic Specific One-off Advanced
Representation technologies	Domain ontology technologies such as RDF Schema, OWL	RDF, OWL , html, xml
Providers	Professionals	Pro-Ams
Maintainers	Pro-Ams	Professionals

2 The infrastructure required to launch the initiative.

This initiative is funded by National Natural Science Foundation of China (Project No. 71103020, Project Leader: Chaolemen Borjigen) as well as National Social Science Foundation of China(Project No. 13FTQ003 and 15BTQ054, Project Leader: Chaolemen Borjigen). It costs more than 470,000 RMB in sum.

The project team mainly consists of researchers from Renmin University of China and Tsinghua University, both of them are China' top universities.

The hardware and software are mainly provided by the Key Laboratory for Data Engineering and Knowledge Engineering (Renmin University of China), Ministry of Education. It is the top laboratory for knowledge engineering in China.

3 The challenges that were encountered, how they developed and how they were overcome.

1. A human-machine cooperative perspective is introduced into KM in order to make full use of the complementary advantages of human beings and machines. There are two challenges faced by the current research on KM: one of them is how to break through bottlenecks in knowledge processing by human beings or machines via lowering the cost of knowledge sharing or innovation as well as adopting machine-understandable knowledge processing technologies; the other is how to make full use of the complementary advantages of human beings and machines by combining those two different KM patterns.
2. Seven key features of knowledge processing on the Semantic Web are identified, and the initiative comes to the conclusion that the Semantic Web provides a new solution to get around the bottleneck of machine's knowledge processing and to establish a human-machine cooperative knowledge processing pattern. The key features of knowledge processing on the Semantic Web are ma-

chine-oriented knowledge representation, computer-readable knowledge networking, computer understandable knowledge rules system, the atomic processing unit, front controls in knowledge processing, integrated with the Web2.0 and its fractal evolving nature. As a result, this project not only deepens theoretical research on the Semantic Web, but also widens practical applications of it.

3. A novel methodology for KM called Mass Collaborative Knowledge Management Methodology (Table1) is proposed in order to integrate the Semantic Web with Web 2.0, and a new model for building the Semantic web-based Organizational Knowledge Ecosystem (Figure1) is also provided, embracing the long tails into organizational knowledge chains in order to nurture a collective intelligent, self organized and meta-synthetic knowledge ecosystem. Further, its object model (Figure 2), interaction model (Figure3) as well as functional model (Figure 4) is also proposed.

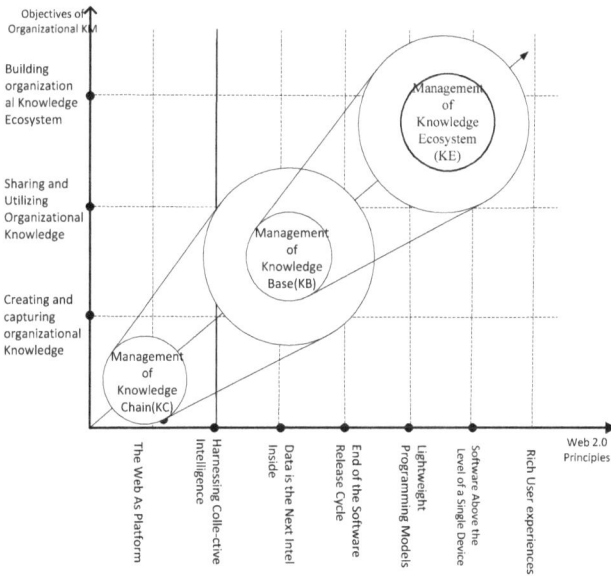

Figure1: A model for building the Semantic web-based Organizational Knowledge Ecosystem

Chaolemen Borjigen

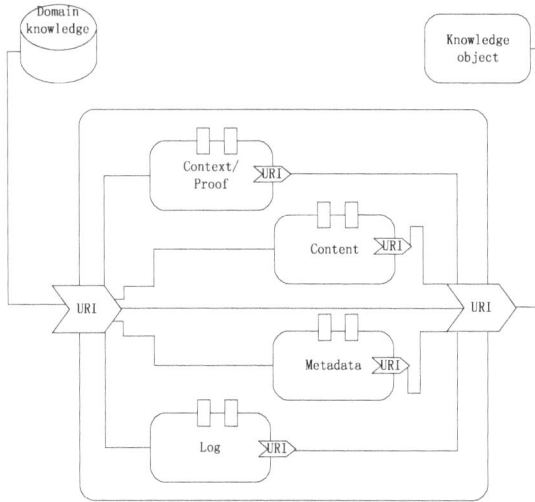

Figure2: Knowledge objects in Mass Collaborative KM

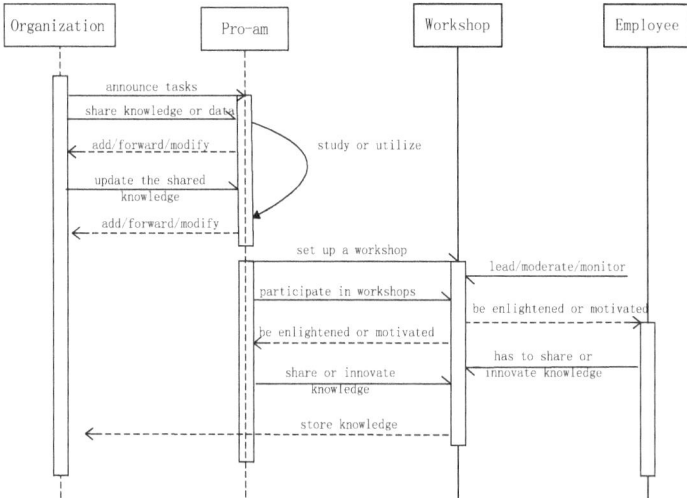

Figure 3 Interaction process within Mass Collaborative KM

48

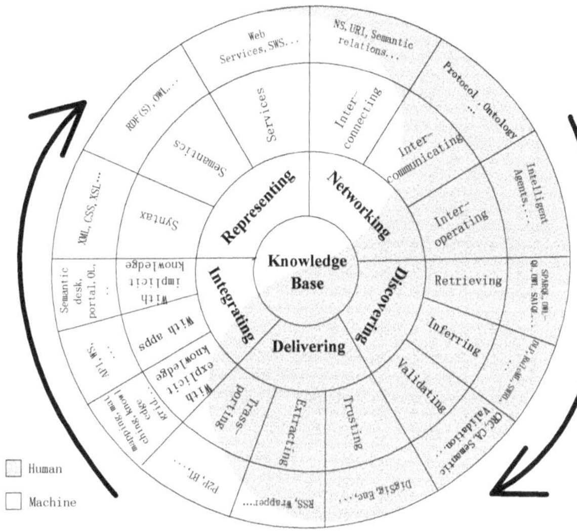

Figure 4: Main functions of Mass Collaborative KM

4. An integrated framework (Figure 5) to provide guidelines on im-plementing knowledge processing applications and to build organ-izational knowledge ecosystems, based upon proposing Semantic Web-based Hall for Workshop of Meta-synthetic Engineering. The whole framework consists of two sub frameworks and an inter-face between them. 1) the sub framework for organizational knowledge processing applications is located at the lower half-part of the whole framework and comprised of four different lev-els: network layer, semantic knowledge layer, computing layer and application layer; 2) the sub framework for organizational knowledge ecosystem, in contrast, consists of application layer, agent layer, workshop layer and social intelligent layer, which are located at the upper half-part of the framework;

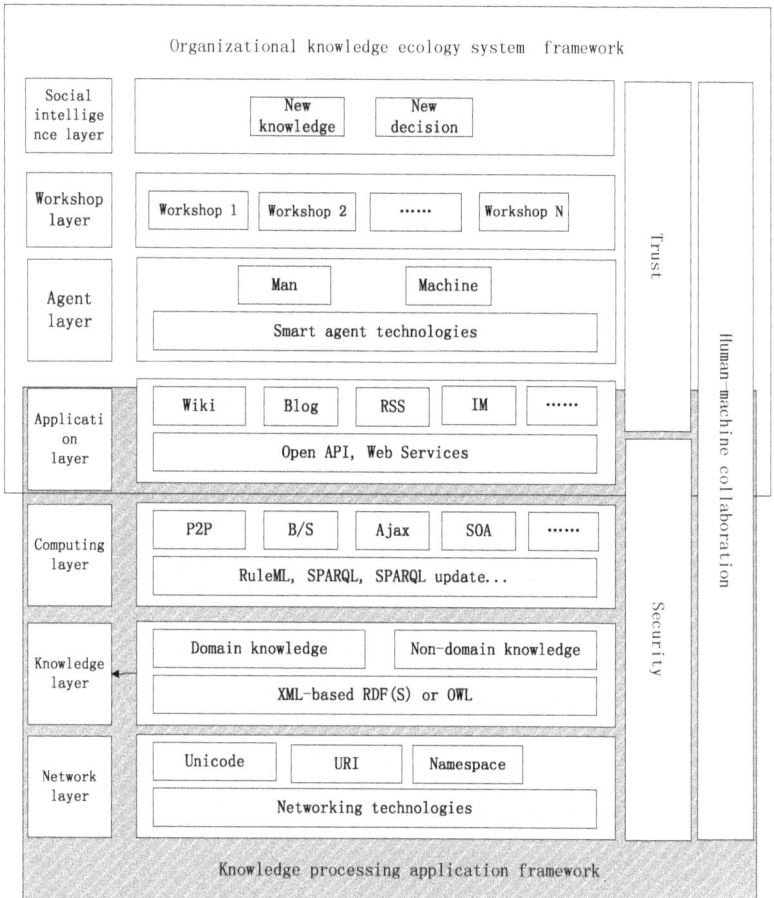

Figure 5 an integrated framework for Mass Collaborative Knowledge Processing on the Semantic Web

3) The application layer bridges the gap between those two sub frameworks and plays a role of the interface between them. This interface layer consumes the services provided by the software sub framework and further provides its services in forms of Web2.0 applications for the ecosystem sub framework. As an interface layer, it possesses the following characteristics: higher ef-

ficiency in knowledge processing by machines in that the Semantic Web technologies are applied in it; higher effectiveness in knowledge sharing or innovating by harnessing collective wisdom, self-organization in Web2.0 based knowledge workshops.

Besides, this initiative applied the following research methodologies:

- **Literature research** is conducted for reviewing state of the art in KM, semantic web-based knowledge processing as well as the relevant subjects, and for identifying gaps prevailing knowledge management theories and the emerging knowledge initiatives such as Crowd Sourcing, Web2.0 and Open Innovation.
- **Case studies** are carried out for describing the emerging features of Semantic Web-based Knowledge Processing. More than 20 knowledge processing projects are investigated in depth for the purpose of revealing the underlying features of semantic knowledge processing applications, including AKT(Advanced Knowledge Technology), Knowledge Web, On-To-Knowledge, Service Web3.0,NeOn,Revyu,SIMILE(Semantic Interoperability of Metadata and Information in unLike Environments), Semantic KiWi, Soogle, Watson, FOAF, Yahoo! SearchMonkey, Microsoft Powerset, Open Calais, DapperMashupAds, KiWi, NEPOMUK(Networked Environment for Personalized, Ontology-based Management of Unified Knowledge), MyGrid, and DBPedia.
- **Knowledge engineering methodologies** are utilized to design the three core models for Mass Collaborative Knowledge Management via integrating Web2.0 with the Semantic Web and proposing the typical workflow of Man-Machine cooperative knowledge processing.
- **Meta-synthetic Engineering methodology, especially the Hall for Workshop of Meta-synthetic Engineering**, which stems from eastern philosophies, **is employed to design the integrated framework** for Semantic Web-based mass collaborative knowledge processing. The construction of that framework also follows the specific rules which are widely used in Computer Science: First, the design of the layers ensures high independence between

adjacent layers, in other words, each layer is in responsible for one specific function. Second, each layer is consuming service provided by its adjacent lower layer and provides its own knowledge processing services to the immediate upper layer. Thirdly, there is an interface layer that will be shared by the two sub frameworks and connects them seamlessly.

- **Software Engineering methodologies** are used to look into the underlying features of the existing Semantic Web applications, to design the sub framework for mass collaborative knowledge processing applications, and to conduct case studies.

4 How the initiative was received by the users or participants.

The initiative was received by the users at two different levels:

1. **Knowledge processing software.** The initiative provides the basic modes for software engineering, including its object model, the interaction model as well as the functional model. Further, a reference framework for implementing applications in compliance with Mass Collaborative Knowledge Management is also provided. Therefore, software engineers can easily build their own applications based upon the modes as well as the reference framework provided by the initiative. Currently, we have successfully implemented two different applications by employing the models and the reference framework: a Semantic Web-based Linked Data Retrieval System (Registration number: 2011SR038833, certificated by: National Copyright administration of China) and a Knowledge Map System for Consulting Companies (Registration number: 2011R011226, Certificated by: National Copyright administration of China).

2. **Organizational knowledge management.** The principles, models and best practices can help an organization nurture its knowledge ecosystem by embracing the long tails and pro-ams into organizational knowledge management by implementing a self-organized and meta-synthetic knowledge ecosystem. One of its typical ap-

plications is iDlib , which is an electronic library implemented by Tsinghua University, has been employed some of those main principles.

It is notable that the initiative provides an integrated top design for organizational knowledge intervention and knowledge processing software. **Therefore, the initiative not only fills the gap between knowledge software system and knowledge ecosystem, but also resolves the conflicts between the volume of knowledge and the formalization of it.** Those practices are leading a revolution in traditional knowledge processing practices.

5 The outcomes that were achieved and how they were measured and evaluated.

The main findings of this initiative involve the design, implementation and applications of the fundamental models for mass collaborative knowledge processing on the Semantic Web.

1. **Defined the fundamental models for mass collaborative knowledge processing on the Semantic Web, including its object model, interaction model as well as functional model.** The object model provides a guideline for how to encapsulate, interlink, province and editing a knowledge object. The interaction model describes the roles of knowledge participants and the collaboration processes. The functional model defines its functionalities and describes the life cycle of knowledge objects at business, knowledge processing and semantic web layer, respectively. (Typical outcomes: 2 patent applications; 2 SSCI papers)

2. **Proposed an integrated reference framework for mass collaborative knowledge processing on the Semantic Web and discussed its operating mechanism.** This framework includes two sub-frameworks: the sub framework for implementing software applications and the sub-framework for implementing knowledge ecosystems within organizations. Further, relevant security and trustiness mechanisms were discussed in great detail. (Typical outcomes: 2 academic books)

3. **Provided the typical applications and cases studies:** Typical knowledge processing systems such as Amazon Mechanical Turk and DBpedia were discussed. Further, a typical application for mass collaborative knowledge processing on the Semantic Web was implemented via OWL/SPARQL/Jena technologies. (Typical outcomes: 2 software copyright, 1 series academic papers)

This initiative will be of great significance for promoting knowledge sharing, building open knowledge ecosystem, and resolving conflicts between the volume and the formalization of knowledge in the knowledge base.

Type: software copyright

Software name: A Semantic web-based linked data retrieval system

Registration number: 2011SR038833

Certificated by: National Copyright administration of China

Type: software copyright

Software name: A knowledge map system for consulting companies

Registration number: 2011R011226

Certificated by: National Copyright administration of China

6 Plans to further develop the initiative.

To put the research findings into more practices and revise them. Although those finding has been successfully employed for several software engineering practices, there are few of practices on building organizational knowledge ecosystem based upon them. Therefore, we will focus on putting those findings to more practices, especially organizational knowledge intervention.

To conduct more in-depth research into some extra topics of Mass Collaborative Knowledge Management, especially on how to build trueness between the participants as well as how to coordinate a mass collaboration intervention. It is also crucial to manage the life cycle of knowledge processing tasks, including to break a knowledge processing task into more of smaller sub tasks, assign them to expected Pro-Ams, track the progress of their completion status, recompose the results of sub tasks into the final results.

Chaolemen Borjigen

Irish Defence Forces' Information and Knowledge Management (IKM) Programme

Barry Byrne
Defence Forces Headquarters, Ireland
barry.byrne@defenceforces.ie

1 Introduction to initiative and its specific objectives.

About Defence Forces Ireland

With an approved strength of 9,500 people, the Irish Defence Forces (DF) is organised on conventional military lines. It is structured with Defence Forces Headquarters (DFHQ), two infantry brigades, a DF Training Centre, Air Corps and Naval Service distributed across 16 installations nationwide and on two major peacekeeping missions overseas in Lebanon and Syria (UNIFIL and UNDOF). The Communications Information Services (CIS) corps, headquartered in DFHQ is responsible for all matters relating to Information and Communications Technology (ICT) nature, both on island and on any overseas deployments.

Today the DF operates in an environment in which knowledge is a primary resource and therefore a key enabler for the conduct of operations. The DF recognised the need to address Information and Knowledge management in response to the rapidly changing information requirements which impact on a modern professional military organisation.

Due to geographic separation at home and overseas, members of the DF could experience difficulty in accessing corporate knowledge and information. The legacy system consisted of internal file shares on a closed network. Emerging technologies and the transition from a paper based to a digital working environment resulted in an exponential increase in information available at all levels and therefore a very real risk of information overload. The DF had a wealth of information that could be identified and classified as corporate knowledge. This information and knowledge needed to be made readily available to all decision makers within the organisation. Key business tasks required rapid access to accurate records, documents and other information of all types and formats. The challenging financial environment prevalent in Ireland places a significant responsibility on DF management to ensure the successful, cost effective delivery of military capability as well as DF business and support functions.

Due to the high volume of information within the DF a new system was needed to improve document management and records management throughout the organisation. The high turnover rate of personnel also meant that intellectual capital needed to be harnessed and preserved so that valuable knowledge did not walk out the door when personnel did. In delivering transformation, the DF embraced a holistic approach to the management of information. The DF improved their Information and Knowledge Management capability in order to provide the right information to the right person, at the right time, to facilitate optimum decision making.

This is the largest knowledge management project of its type in Europe this year, it is based on Internationally recognised academic and empirical research. The Implementation was conducted using cutting edge technology and the project has yielded significant Return on Investment (RoI) and cost saving efficiencies to date; Return on Investment of over €750,000 per annum.

In 2008 the Defence Forces began its multi-year, multi-phase project to address knowledge management in the organisation. A major part of this project was the implementation of an online system which would connect users across the organisation with ease and also provide Electronic Document and Records Management (EDRMS) capability.

The Irish Defence Forces (DF) has implemented a Knowledge Management System based on SharePoint 2013. The new system, Information and Knowledge Online, IKON has improved internal communication, increased productivity and enhanced decision making across all sections of the Defence Forces.

The project also was accompanied by a major change management program aimed at changing the culture of the organisation to a knowledge sharing organisation. This can be seen in the video by senior management to all DF members. (link in email).

Tacit and Explicit knowledge is shared by the use of an 'expert locator' linking the individual with a question to the relevant expert, wiki or blog. IKON provides true enterprise search for all Defence Forces members, underpinned by a well thought-out taxonomy, while also fostering improved knowledge transfer between communities of interest with cutting edge implementation of enterprise social capabilities. IKON provides enhanced knowledge sharing for 9,500 personnel who are operating at home and overseas, facilitating greater and easier access to information which will enable better decision-making in a shorter timeframe, bringing about significant cost, and sometimes lifesaving efficiencies.

The knowledge management project IKON, has been shortlisted for 'Best SharePoint Solution in Europe' (winners announced at the European SharePoint Conference in Stockholm, November 2015 and the project team were awarded IT professionals of the year at the 2015 Technology Excellence Awards in Ireland. The project will be the subject of a 1 hour presentation at the 2015 Knowledge Management KM World conference in Washington.

2 The infrastructure required to launch the initiative.

Planning and training began for the delivery of a DF Information and Knowledge Management (IKM) system to deliver an Enterprise Content Management System for the 9,500 personnel; operating in geographically dispersed locations began in 2008. The Defence Forces sent three person-

Barry Byrne

nel to complete master's degrees in Management of Information Systems and Information Management in Trinity College Dublin and Canfield University, UK.

The DF established an Information and Knowledge Management (IKM) section of five personnel in Defence Forces Headquarters, Dublin. The IKM section, started out by writing the policies and procedures necessary for the culture change to ensure the DF became a knowledge sharing organisation. Together with DF IT Operations, the IKM section then set about creating an IKM portal, entitled DF IKON, (DF Information and Knowledge Online) where the DF's information is created and stored once but is utilised continuously, facilitating extensive sharing and collaboration of information using the Microsoft SharePoint 2013 technology.

This portal provides complete management for the full lifecycle of information and knowledge from creation to archiving or deletion. The solution includes enterprise search, digital records management, enhanced collaboration, internal web content management, document management and enhanced security policy management.

The project team liaised with over 30 organisations who implemented similar projects. The project team linked with information management, lessons learned and training institutions in NATO, the UN and the EU. The project scope included; the establishment of the IKM section, the drafting of the DF IKM Policy and Strategy documents, the preparation and approval at Academic Council of the IKM course syllabi. It also included the procurement upgrade and commissioning of all supporting infrastructure (SAN, server farm, SQL cluster, load balancers, etc.) and software necessary to deliver the project. It further included the training of personnel (over 2000 personnel in 2014 alone) and the continual benchmarking and improvement of the portal and processes that support it against international standards and best practises.

The change management program that accompanied the arrival of IKON was essential in bedding in the idea of knowledge sharing in the Defence Forces community.

Barry Byrne

An extensive awareness campaign was conducted throughout the Defence Forces, at home and overseas. Over 250 'train the trainer' week-long courses were conducted in knowledge management and a further 2,500+ personnel were trained on a one day KM course.

Lessons Learned

A new lessons learned submission and dissemination system, DFKO (Defence Forces Knowledge Online) was built on IKON to specifically focus on the 'K' or Knowledge within IKON. Users required a greater degree of trust to establish documents as corporate knowledge, so a submission and validation system tracks all lessons identified as they pass through the lessons learned cycle. Subject matter experts validate all items submitted before they become visible to the broader community. The same system, built after years of studying similar systems in the civilian world and organisations such as NATO JALLC (Joint Analysis and Lessons Learned Centre), can track contributions to knowledge sharing wikis and sharing knowledge through short 'how-to' video clips.

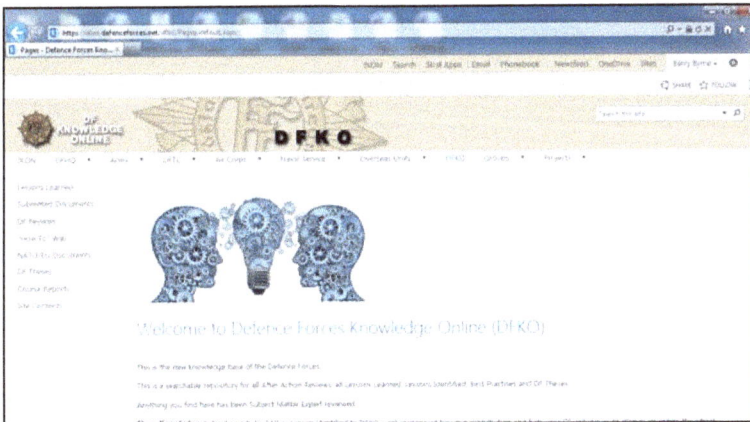

Figure 1: Irish Defence Forces Knowledge Online

3   The challenges that were encountered, how they developed and how they were overcome.

The primary challenge that any large KM initiative faces is resistance to change and the DF IKM programme was no different. The way this was addressed was with first with education; an extensive awareness and education campaign was undertaken across the 9,500 personnel of the Defence Forces.

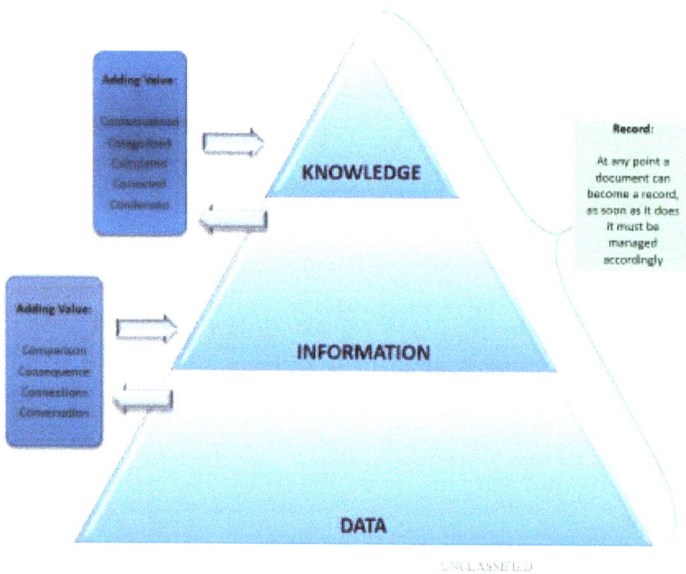

Figure 2: Knowledge, information, data pyramid

Ensuring senior leadership buy in was another way of overcoming resistance to change. The success of this senior leadership buy in can be seen in the press statement issued below, in video messages given by senior leadership and by the engagement of senior leaders in knowledge sharing through new, innovative social tools on the platform.

"This represents a major step forward for the Defence Forces; it will enable both improved communication for our personnel at home and overseas, and improved access to information which will enable better decision-making in a shorter time frame, bringing about significant cost, and sometimes life-saving efficiencies."

Deputy Chief of staff (Support) Defence Forces, Rear Admiral Mark Mellett. DSM

Finally, by using a carrot and stick approach to ensure engagement, the DF was highly successful. The carrot or incentive for engagement was a prize for each brigade's most enthusiastic user. Prizes such as tablet PCs, games consoles or similar, ensured engagement with the new knowledge management platform and indeed made engagement with the social aspects of the platform fun and educational.

Figure 3: The carrot and stick approach

Good governance structures also helped to ensure support and engagement from users. Pictured below is the governance structure introduced for this KM programme.

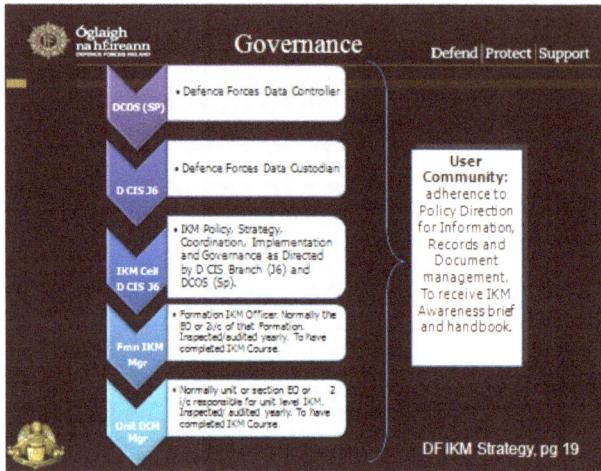

Figure 4: Good Governance structures

Metadata, Ontology, taxonomies, folksonomies, and information architecture were also key to ensuring users could navigate quickly and easily to the correct knowledge or intellectual capital.

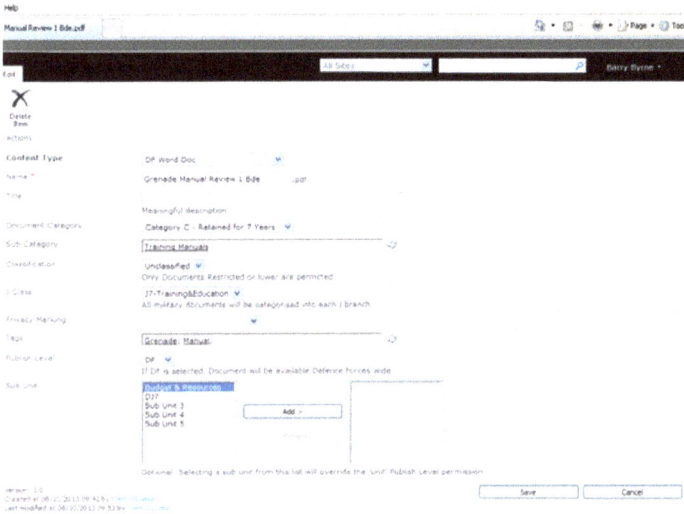

Figure 5: Enterprise search of all knowledge areas, including subject matter experts is presented in an attractive, intuitive interface.

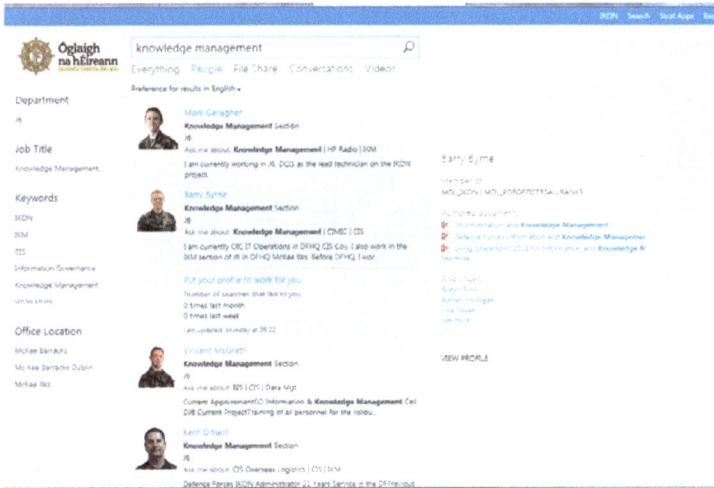

Figure 6: People search results for the term 'Knowledge Management'

By ensuring our people can locate experts on a certain topic, we help tacit knowledge transfer throughout the organisation. Users can also see document authored by that person, thereby accessing freely available explicit knowledge.

All of this work was underpinned by the world leading academic research that was conducted prior to the roll-out phase of the KM initiative.

Research Conducted

Research into this project included three masters' degree theses. Research entitled *Using ICT to Support Information and Knowledge Management in Defence* included over 200 surveys and interviews conducted in; USA, Sweden, Belgium and all Brigades and formations of the Irish DF. Representatives from over 20 Countries and organisations were surveyed; Sweden, Germany, Ukraine, USA, France, Austria, Denmark, Norway, Ireland, Hungary, Canada, Belgium, Malta, Greece, UK, NATO, UN, CIMIC Fusion Centre, LGCSB, Dpt. of Tpt. Dept. Social Protection, etc. This research has been internationally recognised and several papers based on this 1:1 master's thesis, were published and presented in various areas such as the European Conference of Knowledge Management 2013, 2014 the UCD New Ways of War Conference 2011, the Irish Defence Forces review 2013 and the AIIM Conference 2015 in San Diego.

A small sample of some of the findings is provided below;

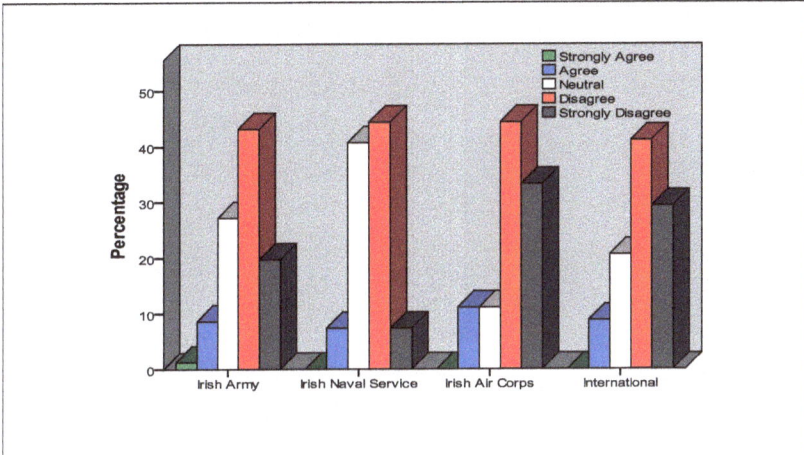

Figure 7: Reward system for positive contribution to the knowledge capital

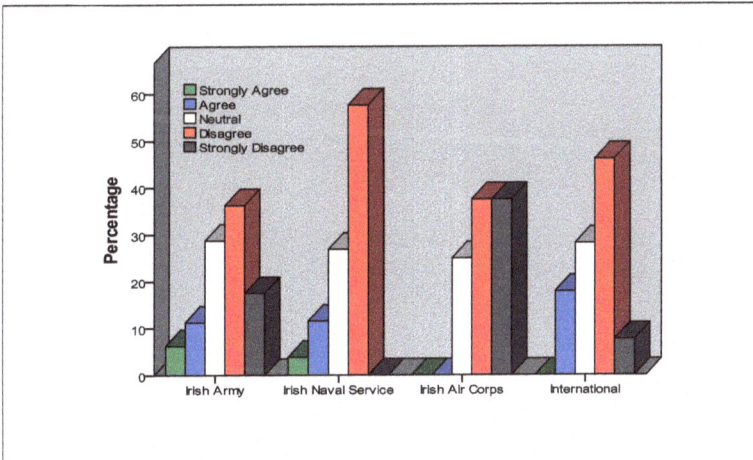

Figure 8: Contributing knowledge and information through DF systems is easy

This extensive research has enabled the DF to avoid some of the pitfalls of other organisations and the project is already becoming recognised as a world leader in the area of IKM and Enterprise Content Management.

This extensive research has enabled the DF to avoid some of the pitfalls of other organisations and the project is already becoming recognised as a world leader in the area of IKM and Enterprise Content Management.

One of the real strengths of the project is the recognition that technology is no *silver bullet* in relation to the challenge of Information and Knowledge Management; significant cultural change needed to take place within the organisation. To this end, the DF IKM Strategy outlines clear governance structures; the strategy has been produced to enable the DF to deliver the technical, organisational and cultural change necessary for the DF to become an IKM leader in the Defence and Security Sector. The strategy states; "It is envisaged that IKM will be introduced in a phased manner such that personnel will change the way they work, and move from a "need to know" mind-set to a "responsibility to share" mind-set. The move to a unified IKM portal has delivered real and tangible benefits for all personnel including; information exploitation, digital records management, cost savings, enhanced collaboration, significantly improved user experiences and significantly improved internal communications. Technology alone cannot deliver the change required. There must be an uptake and buy in by all Defence Forces personnel."

4 How the initiative was received by the users or participants.

The culture change across the DF to a knowledge sharing organisation was significant; expert location, wikis, blogs, online chat and hashtags to follow knowledge topics are all now the norm. The new web solution is important for the DF as it significantly improves communication and workflow amongst its 9,500 members. Intellectual capital is now protected and retained within the organisation as opposed to flowing out as personnel leave.

The new solution now allows members of the Defence Forces to collaborate with troops at home, on Naval ships and abroad on UN mandated peacekeeping/enforcement missions.

The new solution has enabled the DF to deliver the technical, organisational and cultural change necessary for the DF to become an Information Knowledge Management leader in the Defence and Security sector. This has been recognised by many international organisations.

A board of NATO Subject Matter Experts on Information Management moved their annual meeting from Brussels to Dublin to receive briefings and a demonstration on what they consider to be an industry leading system. This had never happened before.

5 The outcomes that were achieved and how they were measured and evaluated.

The move to a unified IKM portal and the introduction of a complete, organisation-wide KM initiative has delivered real tangible benefits for all personnel, including information exploitation, digital records management, cost savings, enhanced collaboration, energy saving, improved user experience and significant improvement in internal communications.

When benchmarked against other militaries, the Irish Defence Forces is one of the leading militaries in the world that has such an up to date platform spanning all of its elements on land, sea and air.

The DF would welcome a site visit to show the judging panel how it's cutting edge use of technology, to enable IKM, is attracting the attention of many larger organisations around the world. A small example of some of these savings is given below. Note that a figure of 3000 PCs was taken for these calculations, not 9,500 personnel, so the figures are very conservative.

6   Plans to further develop the initiative.

This KM programme always had a very well thought-out plan; indeed, rec-
ognising the mistakes made in many KM and ICT projects throughout the
world, from the outset the DF has ensured that this project has real engagement with the business / strategic side of the organisation. This can
be seen in the senior management sponsorship of the project and the fact
that there is an IKM working Group with representation from all key stakeholders within the DF. There is also a very clear roadmap which makes no
apologies for striving to be a Defence and Security Sector leader in the use
of ICT for IKM.

Defence Forces Business Case Assumptions:

Group-Wide User numbers	3,000
Average all-up employee costs / hour	€20.00

Estimated Annual Productivity/Savings	Effective Percentage	Estimated User Numbers	Estimated Number of Projects	ANNUAL Estimated Hours Saved	Incidents per year	DF Weighting	Estimated yearly Gain / Saving
Team portals capture information and provide a virtual collaboration space	50%	1,500		2		1	€60,000.00
Easy and simple web content authoring with approval processes	50%	1,500		1		1	€30,000.00
Improved information dissemination via Discussion groups	100%	3,000		0.5		1	€30,000.00
Improved collaboration and engagment via blogs and wikis	30%	900		0.5		1	€9,000.00
FAST enterprise document search	5%	150		2		1	€6,000.00
Protextion of reputation and sensitive information via comprehensive security controls and self-manageable access rights on content (including search results)	100%	3,000			0.25	1	€15,000.00
Reduction in proliferation of document copies on file shares and email distribution lists and email threads, and associated storage costs	33%	990			0.1	1	€19,800.00
Reduced development and support effort when introducing new services and/or technologies that require integration with messaging and collaboration services (e.g. telephony, unified communications, information management, etc)	100%	3,000	5	0.25		1	€75,000.00
Streamlined manageability of intranet content with functionality to support interactive 2-way communication, and maintain currency and relevance of content	100%	3,000		0.5		1	€30,000.00
Enable general records management and document management to be available to all parts of the business	100%	3,000		0.5		1	€30,000.00
Improved user productivity, experience and satisfaction.	100%	3,000		0.25		1	€15,000.00
Provide a platform on which to implement future network based archiving and data loss prevention services	100%	3,000		0.5		1	€30,000.00
Enable tacit unstructured information to be captured, managed, shared and mined	100%	3,000		0.25		1	€15,000.00
Using the most common platform enables access to a wide range of end user tools, reduced costs of technical skills and choice of service providers	5%	150	2	2	2	1	€24,000.00
Reduction of impact due to High availability solution	100%	3,000		8	0.2	1	€96,000.00
Improve ability to integrate new technologies that integrate with messaging and collaboration services from Microsoft and other 3rd parties	100%	3,000		0.5		1	€30,000.00
Lower costs & improved reputation due to "green" technologies requiring less infrastructure, power & cooling	3%	90	5	1.5		1	€13,500.00
More efficient collaboration: room bookings, on-line conference, shared documents	80%	2,400		1.5		1	€72,000.00
Leveraging the brand and driving employee enthusiasm through deeper and more meaningful connection	100%	3,000		0.5		1	€30,000.00
Improving knowledge, document, people and expertise search across the Defence Forces	100%	3,000		0.5		1	€30,000.00
Creating virtual teams, breaking down silos and bringing HQ closer to the field	100%	3,000		0.5		1	€30,000.00
Targeted and effective information delivery and subscription	10%	300		2		1	€12,000.00
Cost reduction and prodcutivity by reduced use of paper	100%	3,000		0.2		1	€12,000.00
Reduced duplication of information and knowledge	10%	300		2		1	€12,000.00
Enterprise "YouTube" for knowledge sharing	100%	3,000		0.25		1	€15,000.00
Workplace notifications	100%	3,000		0.2		1	€12,000.00
Live Collaboration	10%	300		0.25		1	€1,500.00
Active "sustainability" performance monitoring	100%	3,000		0.1		1	€6,000.00
Secure" printing	10%	300		0.25		1	€1,500.00
Potential ANNUAL productivity improvemetns / cost savings							**€762,300.00**

Figure 9: Business Case Assumptions

Original IKON Excel Project plan.
(Detailed MS Project file available on request)

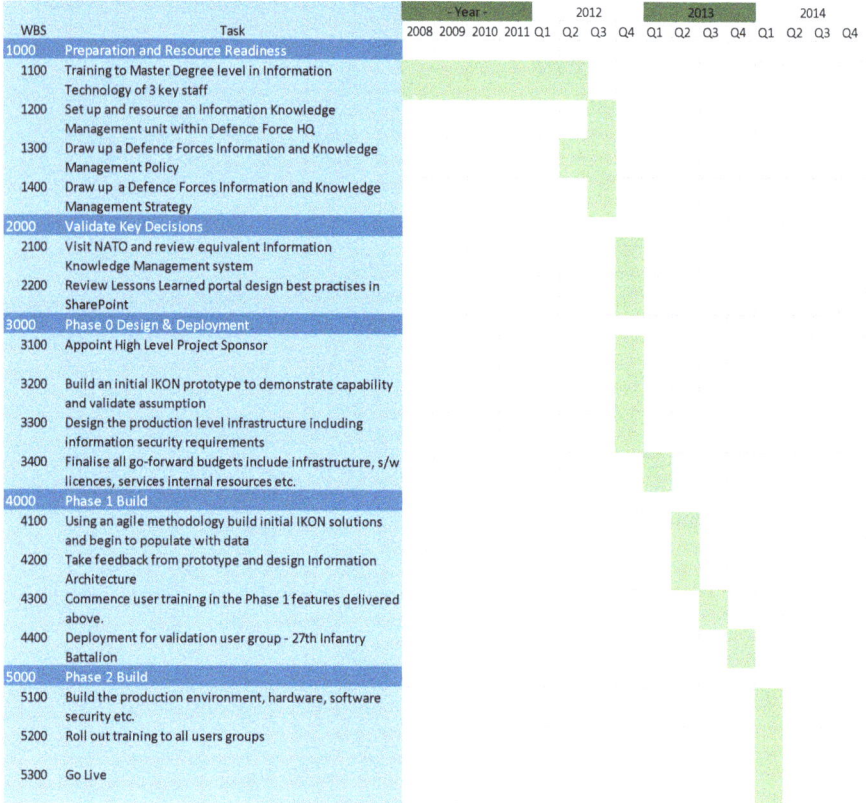

WBS	Task	- Year -				2012				2013				2014			
		2008	2009	2010	2011	Q1	Q2	Q3	Q4	Q1	Q2	Q3	Q4	Q1	Q2	Q3	Q4
1000	Preparation and Resource Readiness																
1100	Training to Master Degree level in Information Technology of 3 key staff																
1200	Set up and resource an Information Knowledge Management unit within Defence Force HQ																
1300	Draw up a Defence Forces Information and Knowledge Management Policy																
1400	Draw up a Defence Forces Information and Knowledge Management Strategy																
2000	Validate Key Decisions																
2100	Visit NATO and review equivalent Information Knowledge Management system																
2200	Review Lessons Learned portal design best practises in SharePoint																
3000	Phase 0 Design & Deployment																
3100	Appoint High Level Project Sponsor																
3200	Build an initial IKON prototype to demonstrate capability and validate assumption																
3300	Design the production level infrastructure including information security requirements																
3400	Finalise all go-forward budgets include infrastructure, s/w licences, services internal resources etc.																
4000	Phase 1 Build																
4100	Using an agile methodology build initial IKON solutions and begin to populate with data																
4200	Take feedback from prototype and design Information Architecture																
4300	Commence user training in the Phase 1 features delivered above.																
4400	Deployment for validation user group - 27th Infantry Battalion																
5000	Phase 2 Build																
5100	Build the production environment, hardware, software security etc.																
5200	Roll out training to all users groups																
5300	Go Live																

Future plans for development

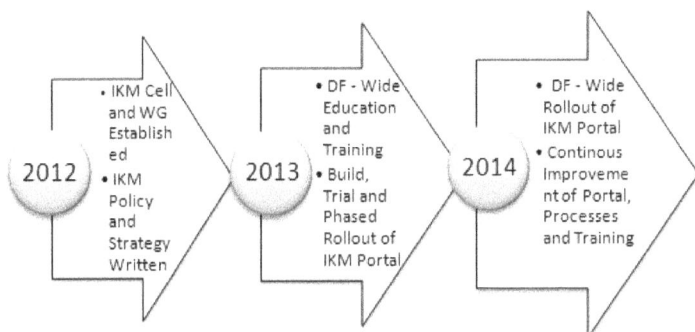

2012
- IKM Cell and WG Established
- IKM Policy and Strategy Written

2013
- DF - Wide Education and Training
- Build, Trial and Phased Rollout of IKM Portal

2014
- DF - Wide Rollout of IKM Portal
- Continous Improvement of Portal, Processes and Training

What the Press said

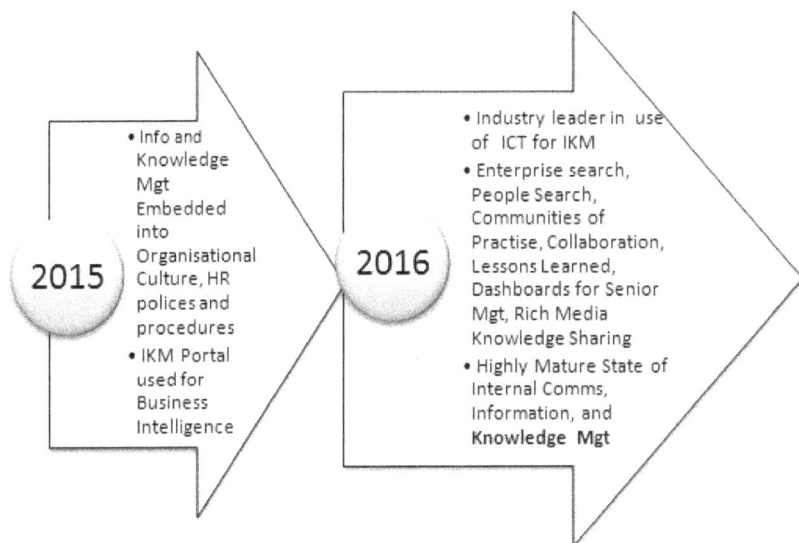

2015
- Info and Knowledge Mgt Embedded into Organisational Culture, HR polices and procedures
- IKM Portal used for Business Intelligence

2016
- Industry leader in use of ICT for IKM
- Enterprise search, People Search, Communities of Practise, Collaboration, Lessons Learned, Dashboards for Senior Mgt, Rich Media Knowledge Sharing
- Highly Mature State of Internal Comms, Information, and **Knowledge Mgt**

A. Appendices:

- http://www.siliconrepublic.com/enterprise/item/36408-irish-defence-forces-in-one
- http://www.techcentral.ie/spanish-point-technologies-aids-defence-forces-ikon-project/
- http://www.wm360.com/news/sharepoint/sharepoint-rolled-out-to-the-irish-defence-forces/
- http://www.spanishpoint.ie/Pages/News/Defence-Forces-and-Spanish-Point-awarded-IT-Professional-Team-of-the-Year.aspx
- http://www.techexcellenceawards.ie/winners/
- http://www.siliconirelandnewswire.com/2015/05/defence-forces-and-spanish-point.html

TechCentral.ie

TechLife TechPro **TechTrade** TechRadio Downloads

Spanish Point Technologies aids Defence Forces' IKON project

Project promises cost savings, greater efficiency

Pictured: Sgt Kern O'Neill, John Corley, Spanish Point and Cpt Barry Byrne

Read More: Deals done Defence Forces IKON Implementations Information and Knowledge Online Spanish Point Technologies

7 April 2014 | 0 Microsoft Certified Gold Partner Spanish Point Technologies is working with the Irish Defence Forces with its ongoing ICT project to deliver Information and Knowledge Online (IKON).

The enterprise-wide system, which consists of a fully integrated Web platform, will improve collaboration and provide information, knowledge, document and records management for all divisions of the Defence Forces (DF).

The Irish Defence Forces has an approved strength of 9,500 members spread across the army, naval service, air corps and the reserve defence forces.

The solution enables members of the Defence Forces to communicate effectively regardless of their geographical location and share information and knowledge on a single unified platform. It will considerably increase productivity and deliver significant

Irish Defence Forces in one of Europe's largest SharePoint deployments

by John Kennedy

Screenshots of KM Solution

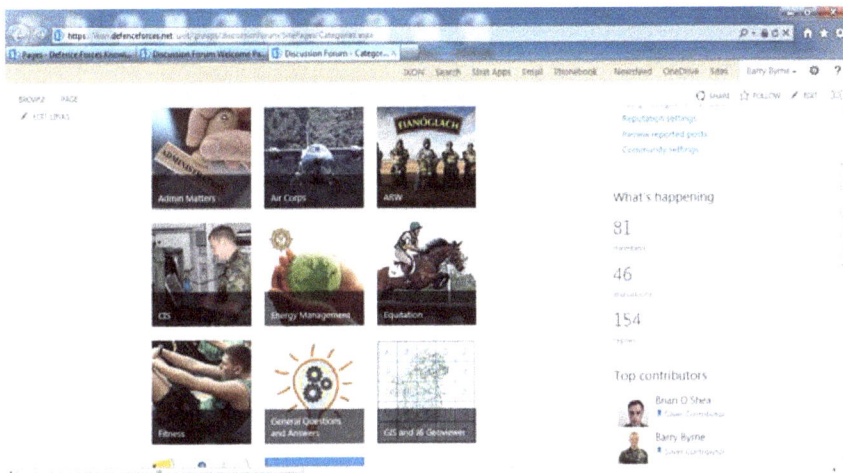

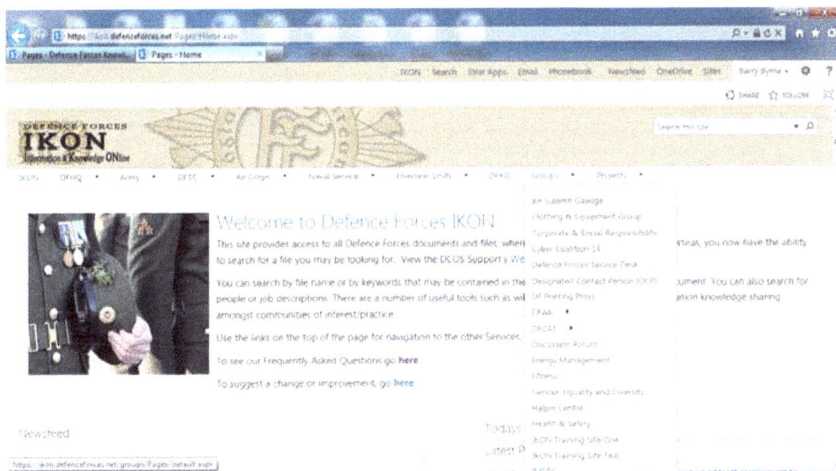

Barry Byrne

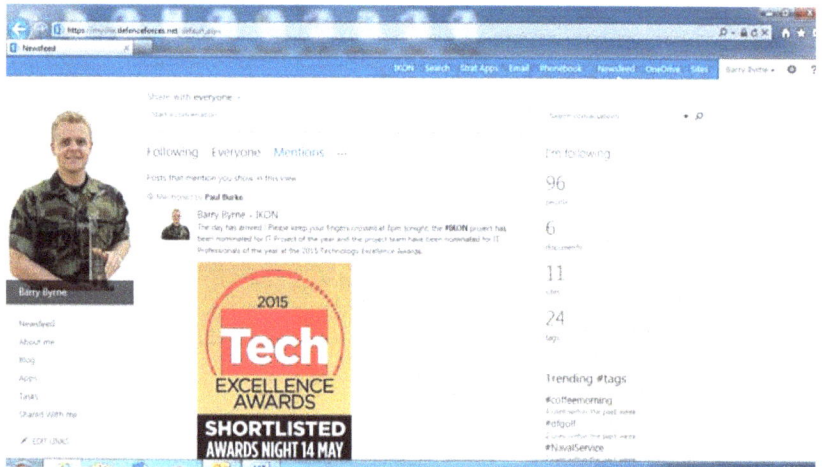

Barry Byrne

Presentation on main stage of AIIM 2015, San Diego

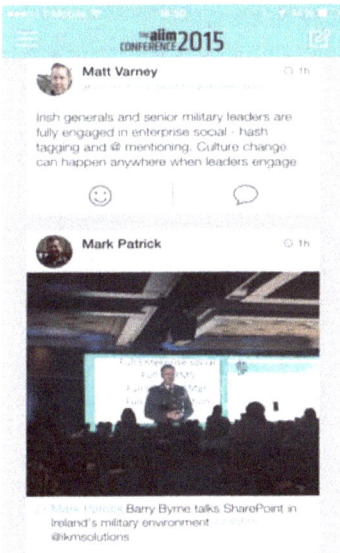

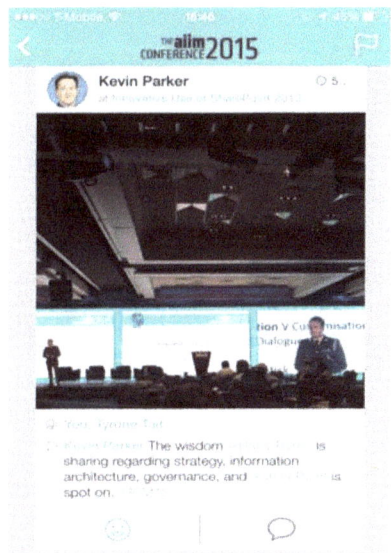

Barry Byrne

My Knowledge: The academic side of corporate knowledge management: The case of My Knowledge

Evangelia Siachou, George Bravos, Dimitris Apostolidis
Hellenic American University, USA

esiachou@hauniv.edu

Abstract

This report refers to the development of My Knowledge initiative, i.e, a Knowledge Management (KM) system that was developed and established in a Higher Education Institution (HEI), Hellenic American University (HAUniv). The nature of the initiative, its main aim and objectives as well as the necessary infrastructure are comprehensively described and discussed in the first two sections. Additionally, issues reflected include: the challenges encountered, the perceptions of the end users towards the development and implementation of the KM system and its efficiency and effectiveness. Plans for further and future development are presented in the sixth and last section.

Key Words: Higher Education Institutions (HEI), Knowledge Management, Knowledge Sharing, Knowledge Processors.

1   Introduction to initiative and its specific objectives.

The applicability of corporate knowledge management (KM) tools and practices in higher education is hard for academics to achieve. One plausible obstacle could be the two types/perspectives of knowledge embedded in Higher Education Institutions (HEI): (i) academic knowledge possessed by the faculty and disseminated to students through learning and (ii) institutional knowledge refers to the overall operation of the Institution (Pinto, 2014). Scholars have also accurately identified a number of negative parameters for the development of an effective KM system in HEI which are linked to the heterogeneous students' profile, cultural differences between the faculty and student body, different learning needs and/or learning styles (see for example, Gupta et al., 2015; Pinto, 2014). However, we challenged the development of a KM system within our HEI that builds on a virtual Community of Practice (CoP) of Knowledge Processors (in our case sources and recipients of tacit knowledge) hence forth referred to as "My Knowledge". This initiative mainly aims at the sharing of tacit knowledge (without ignoring the explicit knowledge embedded in various repositories and data bases of the Institution) outside the class boundaries and beyond the conventional teaching between and within the faculty and the students of an American HEI which also operates in Greece (Athens Campus).

1.1 The nature of My Knowledge

The initiative of My Knowledge derived from the rationale that both faculty and students should interactively communicate on a daily basis inside and outside the conventional and virtual classes. This interaction created the need for a virtual CoP to generate a stock of current unexploited tacit knowledge possessed by the gatekeepers in specific fields (i.e., the faculty). Further to it, the knowledge sharing culture between the main stakeholders (i.e, faculty and students) who interact in both regions (Manchester and Athens Campuses) was supported. The applicability of this initiative was also referred to the case of adjunct faculty who, by the nature of their tasks, interact less frequently between and within the tenures and the students of the Institution. Additionally, as our Institution recently established the eLearning mode for the delivery of classes, the development of My Knowledge became even more necessary for the creation of effective knowledge sharing linkages between and within a virtual community.

Based on the network theory we conducted a social network analysis to identify social networks and relationships (or the lack of them) which resulted in either effective knowledge sharing or knowledge isolation only to those who possess it. The results also enabled us to recognize where the flow of knowledge sharing was disconnected as well as which networks should be added in the processes of knowledge sharing within the CoP.

To that end, the proposed initiative is based on the principles of dynamic communications corporate tools (discussed in the second section). These tools allow Knowledge Processors to participate in virtual knowledge sharing communities developing functional repositories from valid ready-to-use knowledge.

1.2   Aims and objectives

To successfully develop the proposed initiative specific objectives were set to identify (i) the types of knowledge to be shared, (ii) the repositories to store this knowledge, (iii) the appropriate tools for the dissemination of knowledge as well as (iv) accessibility and knowledge value issues. In doing so, we extensively reviewed the extant literature to conclude that the specific objectives of My Knowledge should be set on the grounds of the project based approach (Davenport et al., 1998) rather than the process approach (Demarest's (1997); Galagan (1997); Pedler et al., 1991; Senge, 1992). As such our four certain objectives have as follows:

i.   The creation of knowledge repositories which should include: external knowledge (e.g., competitive intelligence), structural internal knowledge (e.g., research reports, materials, techniques and methods) and informal, internal or tacit knowledge (e.g., know-how and knowledge in specific fields).

ii.   Knowledge access improvement and knowledge sharing facilitation that should secure: connectivity, accessibility, effective sharing tools and appropriate technology to support them.

iii.   Knowledge environment augmentation to facilitate knowledge generation, sharing and utilization that should involve: redesign of the existing organizational processes, new policy as well as the development of related initiatives to support My Knowledge.

iv.   Knowledge stock which should be treated as an intangible asset of which values should be recognized and assessed.

In order to meet these objectives, the University's infrastructure was required and exploited. This multi–dimensional infrastructure is described in detail in the following section (Section 2).

2 The infrastructure required to launch the initiative.

The knowledge management initiative requires several types of infrastructure, including (i) people and expertise, (ii) software and systems and (iii) hardware. The justification of the necessary infrastructure in terms of the three aforementioned categories is made as follows.

2.1 People and expertise

As far as the people and expertise are concerned, My Knowledge requires the support of the gatekeepers (i.e., the HAUniv faculty) and the students (both comprised as Knowledge Processors). These Processors are involved in knowledge exchange activities and operate as sources and recipients of knowledge. Our institution has been a leader in designing and providing higher education services to both undergraduate and postgraduate students. It employs faculty whose core expertise lies in several fields including humanities, business and information technology and art and music to mention a few. It offers over 60 courses in these areas leading to certificates, associates and degree programs. Additionally, we collaborate with European and American Universities offering exchange programs and hosting semester long international study abroad students. As such, significant academic knowledge is possessed by the faculty who play the key role in the development of My Knowledge initiative. The personal/tacit knowledge they possessed is stored in various repositories and categorized based on their expertise. The storage of this knowledge in the appropriate repositories mainly resulting from the students' requests and/or is the outcome of the daily interaction between the faculty and the students.

One of the significant expertise possessed since 2002 reflects the broader characteristics of the suggested My Knowledge initiative. The knowledge required for the implementation of this KM system within the Institution is also derived from our collaboration with the Regional and Local Cisco Networking Academy. This collaboration offers support to other Academies, Instructor and Student Training, and is supplemented by the Apple Authorized Training Center (AATC) operating on Athens Campus. All aforementioned expertise was exploited in the framework of the My Knowledge initiative.

2.2   Software and systems

Our Institution makes use of dynamic communications corporate tools such as the eLearning platform Blackboard (Bb) and Miscrosoft 365 (Student Portal). Their purpose and usability differs as the latter is primarily a repository of Academic and Institutional knowledge. Bb provides 24/7 access to both faculty and students and offers built-in communication tools, such as chat rooms and discussion forums simulating the interaction of a traditional classroom. These tools function as a central hub providing students with the opportunity to place academic requests to the faculty. A well-trained administrator disseminates the requests to the experts who share the knowledge they possess with the interested parties, i.e., the students.

In the case of the Student Portal students are provided access to a centralized repository holding all institutional knowledge including documents, instructions, policies on all actions pertaining to their role as students. Using the functionality of the particular platform, the institution further expanded it usability by providing "blog" space for students to interact and exchange knowledge and place request to faculty. The end user, i.e. the student, has the ability to selectively 'share' the request with the gatekeepers having tagged the request according to key words. A well-trained administrator monitors the flow of knowledge sharing and stores the knowledge to the appropriate repository.

2.3   Hardware

With respect to the infrastructure needs for the implementation of the initiative, HAUniv currently operates 11 classrooms of which 7 are fully–equipped labs with a capacity of 12 trainees, 2 with a capacity of 14 trainees, one with a capacity of 18 and one with a capacity of 19 trainees. Finally, HAuniv has a fully-equipped Apple hardware lab, while the available networking & data management infrastructure includes Cisco 2800 series routers, Cisco 1900 series routers, Cisco Layer 2 & Layer 3 Switches, Cisco Wireless LAN Controllers modules, Cisco Lightweight Access Points, Cisco Wireless PCI adapters, Cisco Soft phone software, Linksys Wireless Access Points and Linksys USB Wireless Adapters.

To that end, HAuniv meets all necessary requirements to support the My Knowledge initiative.

3 The challenges that were encountered, how they developed and how they were overcome.

Challenges were faced during the planning and implementation of the initiative. Specifically, the most important challenge faced in the planning/designing phase of the project was the objective setting. This challenge referred to what should be the aim of a central KM initiative within a HEI framework. Results of three focus groups (two focus groups with the separate participation of faculty and students and one with the joint participation of both) supported by the current literature trends, led us to follow Davenport's et al (1992) project approach regarding the objective setting (see also Section 1.2) as the most appropriate decision path.

Drawing on our initial purpose of the initiative, i.e., to increase the sharing of tacit knowledge between and within the faculty and the students an additional challenge was to find the appropriate manner to execute the generated knowledge stock at the two different levels of stakeholders i.e., faculty and students. Other challenges at this stage included the appropriate technologies, tools and techniques to be developed and implemented as well as their compatibility with the current technological infrastructure supported by the institutional systems. These challenges addressed exploited the expertise, software, hardware, available to the Institution as stated in Section 2. This resulted to reduced implementation costs.

Finally, one should not undervalue the restrictions placed on the initiative as a result of the perception held by both end users and participants. While a challenge, these will be addressed separately in the sections that follow.

4 How the initiative was received by the users or participants.

As already stated, the main stakeholders are (i) faculty (including adjuncts) and (ii) students of HAUniv.

Students strongly supported the initiative as it would enhance their communication with their instructors, while facilitating their accessibility to new and unique academic knowledge. Notwithstanding limited concerns about the knowledge curve involved in learning new components the overall feedback was positive as hey embraced My Knowledge initiative.

Although the development and implementation of the initiative would increase faculty responsibilities and duties the faculty members of our institution recognize early on the added value of the establishment of a central KM system for both academic and administrative purposes.

Special training sessions were organized to help students appreciate the value of a KM system and build a knowledge sharing culture within the HAUniv community. Extensive know how and project implementation expertise positively influenced even the most resisting members of the Community.

5 The outcomes that were achieved and how they were measured and evaluated

My Knowledge is valued as a competitive advantage for the Institution as it both offers storage and accessibility of valuable knowledge stock. Specifically, My Knowledge (i) reduced the cost of unexploited tacit knowledge while at the same time increased the knowledge stock of the University, (ii) improved the knowledge sharing activities between the faculty and the students' body as well as within the faculty and students, (iii) replaced ob-

Evangelia Siachou, George Bravos, Dimitris Apostolidis

solete knowledge with new one and (iv) developed a culture of knowledge sharing within the University apart from the conventional teaching.

As already discussed, one of the main challenges faced throughout the implementation of the initiative was the assessment of the value of My Knowledge. Extant literature supports that the value of an initiative could be measured using the Kaplan and Norton's (1992) balanced scorecard. This tool evaluates based on four main indicators (i.e., customers, internal process, innovation and learning, financial performance) which could determine the added value that My Knowledge has for the Institution.

Initial assessments of the implementation of My Knowledge based on the above mentioned indicators reveled the following institutional value:

i. Customers: increased students' accessibility to unique academic knowledge supplement to conventional teaching;
ii. Internal process: a. decreased knowledge sharing costs through the effective and efficient use of all knowledge sharing platforms (Bb and Student Portal) as well as the institution's infrastructure and human capital, b. improved the interaction between students and faculty and c. generation of knowledge stock ready-to-be used.
iii. Innovation and Learning: offers a new perspective towards learning by enabling students to acquire tacit knowledge without concern of the validity of the accessed information (credibility of sources);
iv. Financial Performance: a. minimizing costs in maintaining large data bases of obsolete knowledge and b. minimizing the costs of acquiring tacit knowledge that was underutilized.

6   Plans to further develop the initiative

Plans for further development of My Knowledge are associated with the basic objectives that have already been defined (Section1.1). Specifically:

Regarding the creation of knowledge repositories, these should include three types of knowledge in total. Up to now, the third type of knowledge (namely that of informal, internal and tacit knowledge) has been successfully developed. Remaining work will focus on the external and structural types of knowledge that exist in the University boundaries. Currently, the priority is on the storage of the structural internal knowledge through the restructure of existing data bases and intranet pages. The storage of external knowledge is planned for the third year of My Knowledge's operation.

Regarding the accessibility issues, further development is planned with the introduction of advanced component permitting end users a more customize experience on knowledge searching and sharing

Regarding the knowledge environment augmentation, the implementation of this initiative is planned to include institutional knowledge managed through the Registrar's and the Academic Affairs Offices with which both faculty and students interact on a daily basis

Regarding the assessment of knowledge stock as an intangible asset we are planning to follow Brroking's (1996) approach that is based on four main modules: market assets, human centered assets, intellectual property assets, and infrastructure assets.

Last, the University plans to conduct a network analysis after two years of My Knowledge implementation, in order to evaluate whether the social networks and the relationships in terms of knowledge sharing between and within the faculty and the students are improved.

Concluding, My Knowledge in its current version provides a promising competitive advantage for the University as it stores, to an extent, important tacit knowledge, that is renewed and maintained without rendering this knowledge unexploited and thus obsolete. Concurrently, it builds a dynamic CoP within a HEI breaking the boundaries of conventional teaching and knowledge ownership. Hence, for HEIs which have the mission to share knowledge by default, My Knowledge is found to be the prerequisite for the development of a knowledge sharing culture which, is by nature challenging to support.

References

Brooking, A. (1996) Intellectual Capital: Core Asset for the Third Millennium Enterprise, International Thomson Business Press, New York.

Demarest, M. (1997) "Understanding knowledge management", Journal of Long Range Planning, Vol. 30, No. 3, pp. 374-84.

Gupta, P., Mehrotra, D. and Sharma, T.K. (2015) "Identifying knowledge Indicators in Higher Education Organization". Procedia Computer Science, Vol. 46, pp. 449-456.

Pedler, M., Burgoyne, J. and Boydell, T. (1991) The Learning Company, McGraw-Hill, London.

Pinto, M. (2014) "Knowledge Management in Higher Education Institutions: A framework to improve collaboration". In Information Systems and Technologies (CISTI), 2014 9th Iberian Conference on (pp. 1-4). IEEE.

Rowley, J. (2000) "Is higher education ready for knowledge management?" International Journal of Educational Management, Vol. 14, No. 7, pp. 325-333.

Senge, P.M. (1990) The Fifth Discipline: The Art and Practice of the Learning Organization, Doubleday Currency, New York, NY.

Lessons learnt from nearly two hundred cases of KM journeys by Hong Kong and Asian Enterprises

Eric Tsui
The Hong Kong Polytechnic University, Hong Kong SAR China

Eric.Tsui@polyu.edu.hk

1 Introduction to the initiative and its specific objectives

The Knowledge Management and Innovation Research Centre (KMIRC) of The Hong Kong Polytechnic University has firmly established itself as one of the principal KM and Intellectual Capital (IC) consultancy and training service providers in Hong Kong and in Asia. Responding to an insatiable demand over the last decade for KM training and consultancy services, KMIRC has played a pivotal role in many KM projects (which many has evolved into a fully-fledged program) in the private sector, non-profit social services organizations and government departments. Through expert advisory and in many cases direct involvement, KMIRC has helped numerous organizations/companies to launch various KM projects, many of which have also taken on our students as interns or even took on our graduates to become members of their KM team. Over the years, close to 200 company-based senior undergraduate, research and consultancy projects have been carried out. The objectives of our centre's work are to

1. Raise the awareness and the importance of managing knowledge at the individual, organizational and societal levels.

2. Assist government departments, private organisations and non-government organisations (NGOs) to introduce and permeate various KM tactics/tools in daily operations to support knowledge-intensive business activities.
3. Perform Benchmarking among comparable organisations and industries to gauge the adoption, maturity and effectiveness of KM, identify good practices, derive lessons learnt to enhance continuous improvement.
4. Provide platforms for effective and regular disseminations of KM trends, good practices, lessons learnt, newly developed tools and techniques among KM researchers and practitioners. Typically, this is being done via seminars, conferences, workshops, webinars, site visits, supplemented by an online repository and various social media channels.

On the type of project, they range from KM readiness assessments, knowledge audit, strategy formulation, taxonomy design and maintenance, cultural assessment and organizational change, knowledge retention from near-retirees, knowledge-enabled business process management, requirements elicitation and selection of collaboration tools including portals, search engine assessments, configuration and continuous improvements, IC reporting and many more. Through implementing custom-developed solutions recommended by the KMIRC, the involved organizations have harnessed and benefited from, among others, sharing of good practices, minimized reinventing the wheel, cultivated new forms of collaborations, enhanced enterprise-wide awareness of information and knowledge, expedited the timely and pro-active delivery of relevant information to staff, customers and consumers, and realized process and productivity enhancements.

2 The infrastructure required to launch the initiative

As mentioned above. KM initiatives and projects which have been introduced by KMIRC for organisations are wide-ranging. For example, common people and process-oriented KM initiatives include

- Cultural and Readiness Assessment
- Formulation of a KM Strategy, Framework & Strategic Planning
- Knowledge Audit and Knowledge Management Audit
- Change Management
- KM Assessment including the definition of metrics and reporting of Intellectual Capital (IC)
- Community of Practices / Special Interest Groups (SIG)

On the other hand, examples of technology-oriented KM projects include

- Search Engine configuration, testing and deployment
- Taxonomy development, maintenance and governance
- Collaboration System(s)
- Enterprise Portal
- Electronic Document Management System (EDMS)
- Knowledge / Information Repositories
- Content Management System (CMS) and Applications (CMA)
- E-Learning
- Intelligent System(s)
- Blogging / Weblogs / RSS Readers / Wikis

Through our work, the involved organisations learnt that rarely a KM project is entirely technical or entire people/process-oriented. In fact, more likely than not, it is an appropriate combination of the above two categories of KM initiatives/systems plus good content management which together form the basis of a KM foundation for an organization. Secondly, KMIRC has also, through a series of carefully devised deployments, demonstrated to organisations that it is highly preferable to commence a KM initiative at a small scale involving business input (e.g. a pilot), then reflect. modify and scale up and/or expand gradually. During the course of the journey, there is often the need for organisations to assess and reformulate the knowledge strategy, to review progress and identify knowledge gaps, to re-assess critical knowledge and flow via knowledge audit and social network analysis respectively for example. Through these efforts and more, participating organisations truly realise that KM is a journey needs to start with a solid foundation/base and evolve from there with

ongoing nurture and support; it should never be viewed/treated as a project (see diagram).

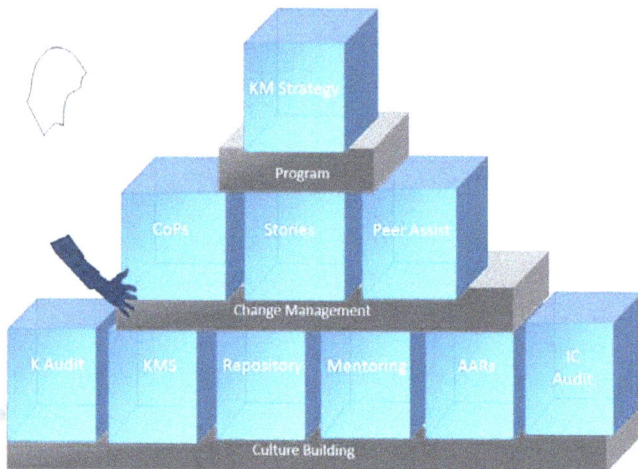

Figure 1: A phased approach to KM with some fundamental building blocks

We are proud to report that all of our client organisations are continuing
with their KM journey ever since the KMIRC introduced and helped them
to kick start their journey. Some organisations regularly seek advice from
KMIRC at different stages of their KM journey. A third point to note is that
KMIRC has also helped to correct many myths about KM including one
which is "KM often needs big investments"; indeed it is possible to start
with a "0 budget KM" journey. Many organisations asked if they need to
set aside large sum of investments (primarily for IT systems/tools) in order
to start their KM journey. KMIRC has demonstrated convincingly that there
is no need to. For example, at the Hong Kong Police where KMIRC staff
trained the Force with the technique of Storytelling (see picture below),
Storytelling sessions are being held regularly among police officers to share
knowledge and experience. At the Department of Health, another client of
the KMIRC, a standard template for documenting meeting minutes incor-

porating a section to record any lessons learnt since the date of the last meeting is routinely being used. Both of the above demonstrate KM technique/process can be permeated into existing daily operations and no separate/additional investments on IT is needed.

Figure 2: Storytelling team at the Hong Kong Police

On resourcing, KMIRC only has 1 full time KM specialist in the team. In all of our projects, we always stress and routinize knowledge transfer with the client. We demand the client to assign resources to work and co-learn together with us; we co-develop and practice the techniques with them and operate with an aim that the organization can plot its own KM course in the medium to long term.

3 The challenges that were encountered, how they developed and how they were overcome.

Many challenges had been encountered and overcome among our 200 or so projects. Many of them are common difficulties that have been reported by western organizations adopting KM. For example, they include difficulty in measuring return on investments, lack of skills and resources to carry out KM projects, how to validate and ensure the quality of the harnessed knowledge, fear of not able to sustain the KM journey etc. but some (e.g. power-distance culture, groupthink, bias on reliance on people/process over technology etc.) tend to be more specific challenges rooted in the Asian culture.

Obviously, it is impossible to list all the challenges that we have confronted at the 200 or so projects but nevertheless I have singled out the following for further discussions:

Table 1: Selection of Challenges

Challenge	Solution(s)
The Business-IT divide – leads to insufficient end-users and Subject Matter Experts (SMEs) input	Create joint teams, group together stakeholders from different departments in a KM project, avoid any single department to be the sole "owner" of a project. Rotate members and expand teams when opportunity exists
Technology is adopted before a strategy has been created e.g. a KM system is installed but it was later found out to be mis-aligned with user's needs	Insist on the formulation of a KM strategy at the early part of the journey. While not always necessary, a Knowledge Audit may be carried out to identify the critical knowledge, the knowledge gap, type of knowledge and the people who create and use this knowledge. Having such information greatly enhance the alignment of any KM tools with user needs. Manage the client's expectation that the strategy and the audit may need to be carried out routinely; they are not a one-off activity
Over-emphasis on KM systems (i.e. the containers), insufficient focus on the knowledge content	Conduct knowledge audit; some knowledge may not be migrated to the new system. Identify critical knowledge assets and develop taxonomies to help categorise the assets in the KM systems
KM is treated/viewed as a project	Demonstrate and convince senior management that recurrent funding is important to support the KM journey as there are on-going needs (e.g. change in external/internal environment) to maintain the taxonomy, content, systems, user learning of new techniques etc.
Poor configuration of the search engine and lack of user training – leads to the under-exploitation of a high power enterprise search engine which has	This is a common problem across many projects. Insist on having regular business input in the configuration, tuning and testing of the search engine; review search engine log to identify improvement areas and set up a governance model to gather feedback, identify and action on improvements on a regular basis. Publishing of

Challenge	Solution(s)
been deployed	usage tips and conduct of user training can also help to raise awareness and usage of high power search engine
Doing KM for the sake of KM	Some clients rush into a KM journey because they were somehow "told" to do KM. This is wrong. In these cases, we performed Readiness Assessment and if there is a strong resentment to adopt KM (for whatever reason), we actually recommended them NOT to proceed with a KM project/journey but to first focus on raising awareness and a change program. It is important to cultivate and gain grassroots support, among other things, to enhance the chance of success of a KM journey
Skepticism about how to monitor and govern the use of Web 2.0 tools for bottom-up knowledge sharing	Advised organistions to adopt WIKI and RSS (rather than blogs) for trials inside the organization. WIKIs are used to foster inter-departmental collaboration on compiling complex, de-centralised documents for example. RSS is adopted to keep up information awareness on specific topics; feeds are calibrated to deliver new and relevant information to individuals, teams, groups, and the entire organization, usually via the Enterprise Knowledge Portal. As these two types of Web 2.0 tools can be easily aligned to support collaborative work and learning (and information awareness), they are seen as easy entry points for introducing Web 2.0 into the workplace. Once knowledge and confidence are gained, other Web 2.0 tool can be explored for adoption
Capture and share tacit knowledge in processes	With input from the Business and IT departments, KMIRC has helped organisations to customize their Electronic Document Management System (EDMS) or Business Process Management System (BPMS) thereby requiring users to codify and record the tacit knowledge behind their decisions into the system so that other users can better ascertain the chain of reasoning throughout the execution of a business process.

Learning has no boundaries. KMIRC has adopted the principle of treating the real world as an "Open KM Laboratory", the learnings from the consultancy and research projects in the KMIRC often become highly regarded teaching materials and industry case studies which are used throughout the Master of Science in Knowledge Management programme. Doing so substantially enhances the sharing of practice knowledge gained from the trenches.

4   How the initiative was received by the users or participants?

As mentioned above, once started, all of the clients of KMIRC continue with their KM journey. This is the strong evidence that KM is yielding good value/return in these organisations. For some organisations like the Hong Kong Police and CLP Power, they have been adopting KM for nearly a decade and are often seen as role model in the public and private sector respectively in the region. MTR, the local train company, has been operating their KM and Innovation program for more than 6 years and has the largest (with around 10 full time staff) KM team in Hong Kong. These companies have great commitments in their KM efforts. Over the last decade, we can further derive the following observations on organisations in Hong Kong that have adopted KM:

For organizations which are *new* to KM, their focus are on

- Awareness raising / Readiness Assessment
- Strategy Formulation / Strategic Planning
- Identify, rank and pilot of KM initiatives
- Knowledge Audit, Social Network Analysis
- EDMS, Search engine, portal deployment
- Taxonomy Creation and Maintenance

For organizations that have *already started* KM, their focus are principally on

- Sustainability of KM programs, culture building
- Strategy revisit, gap analysis
- Embodiment of knowledge in business processes
- Knowledge distillation and harnessing
- Soft KM tools/skills
- Health checks & Benchmarking

Eric Tsui

Additional independent evidences of user adoption, KM advancements and successes among organisations that KMIRC have helped include

- In the last 5 years, many Hong Kong organisations are recipients of the MAKE award, a de facto industry award in KM at the city, regional and global levels. These organisations include Hong Kong Police, MTR Corporations, CLP Power, Towngas, Efficiency Unit of the HKSARG, Arup Ove, and others. Clearly, their achievements are being recognized and endorsed worldwide by independent and vigorous assessments
- Leaders of the KM journey in the above organisations and more are highly sought speakers in the Asia Pacific KM circuits for their sharing of success, good practices and lessons learnt from their KM program; many other organisations in the region are looking to these HK organisations as role models to follow
- A considerable number of staff from the above organisations and more come to KMIRC and PolyU for further training and learning in KM, either supported by the organization or at their own expenses. These people have shown genuine interest and passion in KM
- KMIRC has trained over 2000 professionals in industry and government sectors on KM in the past decade
- Over the years, various Commissioners and Assistant Commissioners of Police have publicly thanked the KMIRC for helping the Hong Kong Police in its KM pursuit
- The writer (Eric Tsui) has been appointed a KM advisor to the Hong Kong Police College by the Commissioner of Police since May 2011 as well as a Community of Practice advisor to the Efficiency Unit (another HK government department) since May 2015.
- More than a dozen of the KM officers/managers/directors in Hong Kong are current students and graduates of PolyU's Master of Science in Knowledge Management program

Many KM luminaries noticed and asked "KM is always active and thriving in Hong Kong. What is the magic formula? Of course, full credits go to the organisations that have committed resources and are patient about returns from KM. We like to think KMIRC also has a role in this, however. Patrick Lambe, 2 times past president of iKMS (Singapore) summarized it nicely in one of his blog articles

"Even more interesting was the turnout at KMAP (a KMIRC-hosted event) last week. At its peak, there were close to 700 delegates in the conference hall during the keynotes day – this is a number unmatched in Asia for a straight KM conference as far as I know – and though it's got a steady and growing range of KM initiatives in both public and private sectors, Hong Kong is not generally noted for its KM enthusiasm. Previous KM conferences in Hong Kong have drifted around the 100 participants mark.

Of this number perhaps a quarter were from public sector organisations in Hong Kong, demonstrating a growing interest there. But there were also delegates from private sector companies and delegates from mainland China, Malaysia, New Zealand, Iran, UK, USA, Finland, Sweden, Germany, and Australia. Some of this diversity is what you'd expect from an academic conference, it's what universities can contribute to the conference scene.

But the particular strategy and role of the HKPolyU also played a significant role, I believe. HKPolyU (more precisely the Dept of Industrial and Systems Engineering) is unusual among universities with KM on their agendas. They do research, and they have a Master's in KM course, to be sure, as do other universities. More than that, however, their KM group has been aggressively building a strong KM consulting practice in both private and public sectors – not as sidelines for their professors and teachers, but as a kind of action research learning experience for both the clients and the KM group itself.

This is interesting. Most KM consulting work is done, to be frank, in secret. Organisations are frequently uncertain about their KM pathways, and often reluctant to share until they have some results. Similarly, private sector consultants tend not to want to share until

their assignments are complete and they are confident of keeping competitors at bay. This means that in novice KM markets, KM activity is opaque, and it's hard for beginners to see many visible examples of KM in action. This multiplies the initial uncertainties and hesitancies. In an action research kind of context with a university, the picture – at least in Hong Kong – seems to have shifted. KM work becomes more visible, so onlookers are encouraged to explore and experiment. This is a major factor, I believe, behind the strong turnout at KMAP – there are now sufficient visible projects associated with HKPU to become, in themselves attractors for attention and networking."

(Source: http://www.greenchameleon.com/gc/blog_detail/universities_and_km_practice/)

5 The efficiency, effectiveness or competitive advantage outcomes that were achieved and how they were measured and evaluated.

Overall speaking, KM initiatives help to accomplish some/all of the following. In term of enhancements and improvements, good KM leads to increase in

- Sales
- Customers
- Quality of decision making
- Consistency in process executions
- Organisational Memory
- Social and Professional Networks
- Response time
- Flexibility in time and delivery channel
- Knowledge about customers, partners, market

and reductions in

- Time to search for information
- Time/Effort needed to locate/connect with knowledge experts

- Time to carry out "knowledge-intensive" tasks
- Time/Effort needed to resolve a problem
- Printing and mailing costs
- Travel cost and time
- Costs of providing training and learning programs

As the number of projects/journeys is close to 200, it is impossible to list out all the details. Nevertheless, the following table provides a subset of the various KM initiatives that have been introduced in organisations, together with its outcomes, measurements and evaluations

Table 2: Subset of KM Initiatives

Initiative/ Tecnique/ Tool/ System	Outcomes	Method of measurement/evaluation
Taxonomy creation and Search Engine customization	Improved schema for storing information; common consensus among staff on where to save/find information; enabled faceted search and enhanced the ranking of search results in the display	Complexity of the taxonomy in terms of levels, no of branches, levels and the size of the controlled vocabularies Reduced time to search for information, both for the navigation method and keyword searching More intelligent search engine that identifies synonyms, recovers from incorrectly typed words Monitor and analyse search engine log for entered keywords with no matches; reviewing this on a regular basis can provide valuable information to fine tune the taxonomy as well as the search engine configurations
Near-miss reporting database	Overcome people's reluctance to report nearly occurred accidents in hospitals. Culture change. Design and development of a database capturing near-miss cases reported from and shared	The steadily growing size of the database Frequency of access and download of these cases from the site Survey on the rise in awareness and usefulness of the database for accident preventions A culture among staff to willingly report near-miss cases with fear of repraisals

Initiative/ Tecnique/ Tool/ System	Outcomes	Method of measurement/evaluation
	among 10 hospitals	
Revamp of a Knowledge Portal	Re-design of the user interface, the layout and content of the portal, introduction of Web 2.0 tools (Wiki and RSS) to enhance collaboration and information awareness, change management to help users adopt the portal	User-adoption statistics Reduced time on the retrieval of information and documents from the portal Refined and more accurate search results from the search engine Monitoring and review of the search engine log to identify abnormal search queries and common keywords encountered but not adopted in the taxonomy Governance model established to review, discuss feedback on a regular basis and action on improvements
Scenario-based E-Learning tool	Developed a platform for rapid authoring of scenarios to support learning using open source tools	Successful adoption of this tool by MTR Corporation and the Langham Place Hotel for internal training purposes Both organisations continue to develop and update the learning content over the years. This is evidence of sustained usage of the tool MTR Corporation also uses this tool to provide videos to help drive change in their KM journey. More specifically, the tool is used to produce videos showcasing why new joiners and junior staff should active ask questions and share in the Community of Practice forums
Knowledge Audit	Identified a ranked list of important explicit assets. Knowledge flow in the audited processes showing the creater/owner/originator/user of a knowledge asset. Social networks revealing connections among people involved in the audited processes and any major knowledge centres (people and reposito-	Verified list of critical knowledge revealed by the Knowledge Audit by Subject Matter Experts in the organization Followup interviews with stakeholders especially to validate some unusual findings in the Knowledge Audit Adopted different methodologies for Knowledge Audit to benchmark findings and identify variations Carry out Knowledge Audit periodically to obtain updated information to support decision making on KM strategies, systems and processes

Eric Tsui

Initiative/ Tecnique/ Tool/ System	Outcomes	Method of measurement/evaluation
	ries, where others approach for information) in the network	
Formulation of a KM Strategy	SWOT analysis from a knowledge perspective The balance between the use of codification and personalization approach Identification of appropriate soft and technical KM tools to support the set KM objectives Recommendation of pilot projects with timeframes and as part of a multi-phased approach to KM	Organisations proceeded with the pilot projects; start small to embark on their KM journey Depending on the KM initiative, for Community of Practice, measurements are based on the number of members, rate of membership growth, no. of assets uploaded/downloaded. For discussions, measurements are often based on threads posted, no of replies and time lag for the reply, the nature of the reply etc. Revisit the strategy to determine its ongoing appropriateness and effectiveness; gap analysis to determine if the strategy and its implementation need to be re-aligned
Stories database	Elicited stories about a given theme/topic are transcribed into a database. Indices and keywords are created to tag these stories for easy and fast retrieval	Stories are verified by the tellers before they are being finalized Measurements include the number of stories elicited, the percentage of stories deemed to be admissible to the story database (for its completeness, integrity and perceived usefulness), organization continuing efforts to adopt storytelling and stories as knowledge harnessing and knowledge sharing methods Anecdotal feedback on the usefulness of the collected stories; comparison of the revealed knowledge with existing training materials and also monitor the access/retrieval of the stories for training and learning purposes

6 Gap between KM in the books and in practice

Have done close to 200 KM projects, one can clearly identify several major areas where KM theories (as covered in most KM books) and practice differ, as well as those practical issues that are not commonly addressed but nevertheless important. We have again summarized the discussions into the following areas:

Knowledge Audit and Knowledge Strategy: Which one comes first?

It does sound like a "chicken-egg" situation. Our experience is that either one can come first, depending on the situation. For example, a century old engineering organization wants to harness and better retain and share their critical knowledge. In that case, almost certainly the team of experienced engineers would know about their core area(s) of expertise and how these are related to the achievement of corporate objectives. However, a Knowledge Audit may not only reinforce what the engineers believe but also provide evidence-based support for specific additional critical knowledge areas/assets that should also be harnessed, retained and shared. The knowledge strategy can come second after the identification of critical knowledge assets. On the other hand, for an organization that is entirely new to KM, it is sensible to first derive a KM strategy then proceed to carry out pilot projects so identified in the strategy. There is no definitive right or wrong decision on choosing which one to proceed first; it determines on the needs and priority of the client organization.

KM journey are rarely started from scratch

Organisations and societies evolve all the time. Therefore, there is rarely the case that an organization truly begins its KM journey from a "clean sheet of paper". This starting point is often ignored in books as KM strategies and operational steps outlined in books tend to assume the journey starts from scratch. The reality is the organization may be already doing something related to managing knowledge but not called it KM. Worse, an organization may have introduced KM before but, due to whatever reason, the journey failed and had poor ramifications among staff. Whatever the case, an organisation's past efforts on KM need to be understood and factored into the strategy for implementation. Our experience is that, more likely than not, there are knowledge assets to filter out and migrate, methods and/or processes to fine tune, culture building among staff, sceptics to deal with, among others, before a journey can move forward. In other words, all organisations have "baggage" that need to be dealt with and cannot be ignored when enacting change.

Natural KM "entry points" in organisations

Although it is never easy to convince someone to adopt KM let along embarking on a KM journey, nevertheless, we found that there are natural "entry points" for organizations to take up KM. These entry points are so natural and almost need no further substantiation. One entry point is when organisations realise their staff is wasting substantial time every day in finding/searching things but to no avail; a taxonomy project can help here. Another one is the global phenomenon of the Babyboomere Retirement Syndrome which refers to the over-proportion of retirement from organisations since 10 years ago and will continue into the next 5 years. No organization is immune from this exodus of staff and no doubt leaders would be receptive to adopting any KM method that can help to reduce some of the lost knowledge by retaining them in knowledge repositories as well as the heads of the remaining staff.

KM strategies vary among MNCs, local companies & SMBs

We also found that there are substantial differences among the adoption of KM in MNC (multi-national corporations), local companies and SMBs (small to medium sized businesses). Especially for those MNCs where their headquarters are in USA or Europe, deployment of KM in local region/offices is typically a rollout or extension of a KM program (including strategy, system, blueprint, operational groups, communities etc.) that is being handed down from their headquarters; the local team's responsibility is basically to operationalize the program with some minor fine tuning or variations. For local (large) organisations, their adoption of KM has, in most cases, a good alignment with the typical KM journey as prescribed in books and literature. For SMBs, due to a lack budget, multi-skilling of staff, and the proprietor's dominance in decision making, their KM journeys need the most vigorous ROI (return on investment) and the course of the KM journey can change radically due to, among others, staff departure, change of decision by the proprietor, market volatility, business performance, skills and competencies of staff and their ability to learn new things.

Factors for sustaining the use of KMS different from factors that affect adoption

KM books and research papers cover extensively the topic of KMS adoption and that is the factors that influence users to take up and start using a KM system. While knowing these factors are no doubt very useful for planning and the deployment of a KM system, it is even more important to know the factors that lead users to continue their use of the KM system in a sustained way. Our own research as well as knowledge gained from working with these 200 projects lead us to believe that the two set of factors (i.e. for pre-adoption and post-adoption) are different, For example, peer influence, demonstrated usefulness, personal experience, personalisation are among factors that lead to users to continue their use of KM system in a sustained way.

IC is much harder than KM to sell

Among the 200 or so projects conducted, a small number of these projects are Intellectual Capital-related projects. Overall speaking, we found that compared to KM, it is more difficult to convince directors to adopt IC project possibly because IC is very new (as many organisations are only just starting to use the Balanced Scorecard for reporting and tracking performance) and that the benefits of IC is not immediately realizable. There are, however, a few major organisations leveraging IC for value creation, reporting and business planning. More time is needed to determine whether IC is a lift-off in Hong Kong or not.

An earlier version of the author's presentation on this topic is available for replay at:
http://158.132.103.175/temp/eric/KM%20developments%20in%20HK%20-%20over%20100%20projects/

Eric Tsui

The Germany ICS initiative: Experiences from more than 10 years of ICS – Made in Germany

Sven Wuscher[1] Manfred Borneman[2], Erik Steinhöfel[1], Ronald Orth[1]
[1]Fraunhofer Institute, Germany,
[2]Intangible Assets Consulting GmbH, Graz, Austria

sven.wuscher@ipk.fraunhofer.de

Abstract

Since the acknowledgement of Intellectual Capital (IC) as a major driver of organizational competitiveness and innovativeness, numerous scientific models and practical approaches have been developed. In this context, an international research
team under the leadership of Fraunhofer IPK carried out the German pilot project
"Wissensbilanz – Made in Germany" (FMET, 2004) as well as the European pilot-
project "Intellectual Capital Statements – Made in Europe" (European Commission,
2008). The pilot projects led to results like the ICS toolbox software and a guideline
for implementing ICS in organizations. In addition, the initiative established more
than 400 trained ICS moderators who are now supporting companies in analyzing
and managing their IC on a high quality level. As the project results were public and
the awareness of companies was growing due to transfer activities, one of the main
challenges was the quality assurance of ICS implementation. For this reason, the
Fraunhofer Academy established an ICS training program for ICS moderators and
an ICS audit system for implemented ICS in companies. Additional challenges of the
initiative were the definition of interfaces to other management concepts like
strategy development, quality management, knowledge management and external
communication. Against this background, different guidelines and support material
for a practical integration of IC management into existing management concepts
were developed.

All together the initiative reached more than 1.0000 companies, who implemented ICS according to the developed methodology all over Europe. In Germany, most of the moderators are organized in a national IC Center which organizes public ICS roadshows, fosters research activities and promotes the transfer of the methodology into teaching programs of universities and to other countries with the aim of developing national IC infrastructures. Promising experiences in establishing national IC structures based on the German framework had been already made in Malaysia, Brazil, Poland, Lithuania, Spain and France.

1   Introduction to the – made in Germany

When the German Ministry for Economic Affairs planned to establish the initiative "Fit für den Wissenswettbewerb" (2004-2011) in 2002, other countries already gained substantial experiences in the field of Intellectual Capital, Intangible Assets and Knowledge Management. Large and important institutions such as the OECD (1996, 1999), the World Bank initiated academic conferences to explore concepts and early experiences in indentifying, measuring and reporting as well as managing and leveraging Intangible Resources of the Knowledge Economy.

The academic literature (e.g. Mouritsen, 1998; Petty and Guthrie, 2001) built on the distinction made by Edvinsson and Malone (1997), Stewart (1997), Nonaka et al (1991) and Sveiby (1997) between three dimensions of IC: human, organizational and customer capital. In the early millennium, maybe starting with the "Danish Guideline" (Danish Agency for Trade and Industry, 2000).

One of the pioneering organizations to adopt Intellectual Capital Statements was the Swedish insurance company Skandia. Edvinsson built on work by the Swedish community of practice for knowledge management, the Konrad Group organized by Sveiby (1986) as well as on the concept of Balanced Score Cards (Kaplan and Norton, 1992), originally established to support implementation of strategic management. The concept was – following the ideas of classic strategic thinking (Whittington, 2001) – focused on communicating the strategy and strategic objectives for each department **top down**. The top down approach supports a specific idea of men and can be described with McGregor (Theory X, 1960), where an elite conceives a strategic plan and employs various resources – in this case: financial resources and infrastructure, both tangible resources, and intangible resources such as human, organizational and customer capital – to generate additional value.

This approach was, of course, not taking advantage of the potential contributions of "knowledge workers" (Drucker, 1991), who might prefer ideas of Theory Y (McGregor 1960), particularly the focus on participation and interdisciplinary decision finding. It took two more approaches to overcome these restrictions. The center of activities shifted from the Nordic countries to Austria.

The Austrian Research Centers Seibersdorf (ARCS, now Austrian Institute for Technology, AIT) were funded by public and private sources. In the last years of the millennium, the institute reported regularly negative financial results. The director for scientific affairs, Günter Koch, thus urgently needed a new form of reporting that better helped to explain the business model and productivity of a research organization. He formed a task force to collect already existing experiences from Scandinavia, particularly from the Danish Guidelines (Danish Agency for Trade and Industry, 2000) and American literature. The result was a model as well as a report "Wissensbilanz 1999", with **strong emphasis on strategic knowledge objectives** derived from the corporate strategy and research programs (Leitner, 2005). Following the state of the art, various indicators were developed to document the status quo of scientific productivity. One of the most prominent indicators became the "number of academic publications". Other figures in the context of "gender and diversity" were interpreted in their impact on innovation and learning. And "new employees leaving the company within 2 years" should indicate potential negative developments in the corporate culture. An extensive text helped to interpret the indicators and create shared context – a feature, which was lost in the next stage of development.

In order to improve thrift and frugality in public funded universities, the concept of "Wissensbilanz" was quickly adopted by the Austrian Government to monitor the performance of Austrian Universities. A task force led by Titscher and Biedermann (2000) suggested an **indicator based approach**, which – after years of fierce academic discussions, changes and refinements – became obligatory for all universities in 2007 (UG 2002). The problem still unresolved was the idea that it is possible to use a set of indicators for any academic institution, independent of scientific orientation, maturity level (at that time, the Bologna Process aimed to structurally reform the academic institutions all over Europe) or strategic focus.

Parallel to these developments, industry adopted the ideas on innovation and knowledge management. In order to make IC manageable in a systematic way, different national approaches on IC measurement and reporting have been developed and tested in recent years, leading to the fact, that there is no world-wide standard regarding the measurement and disclosure of IC. One of the most important reasons for a missing consensus is a conflicting view on IC being displayed in standardized quantitative terms on the one hand and the description of IC according to the individual business strategy on the other. The emerging need for a consistent methodology has been the starting-point for the German pilot-project "Wissensbilanz – Made in Germany" (Alwert et al., 2008) and the European research project "Intellectual Capital Statement – Made in Europe (InCaS)" (Mertins et al., 2009).

2 The required to launch the initiative

As the project coordinator of these German and European initiatives, the "Arbeitskreis Wissensbilanz" under the leadership of Fraunhofer IPK was not only being responsible for the development of the state-of-the-art, the workshop procedure and the software tool, but has also gained comprehensive practical experiences in applying the method in various contexts, from start-ups, small and medium-sized enterprises (SME) to large organizations, research institutions and technology parks.

The structural model of the ICS approach – a result of the consolidation process of international approaches on IC management and reporting – describes the main elements of the ICS as well as their interrelations (see Figure 1). The model is a holistic and systemic representation of the way the organization has structured its business processes to deliver value to the customers. Starting point is the vision and strategy of the organization with a view on the possibilities and risks encountered in the external business environment. Following the most frequently used structure to describe IC, the ICS methodological framework divides Intellectual Capital into the three dimensions: Human Capital (HC), Structural Capital (SC) and Relational Capital (RC).

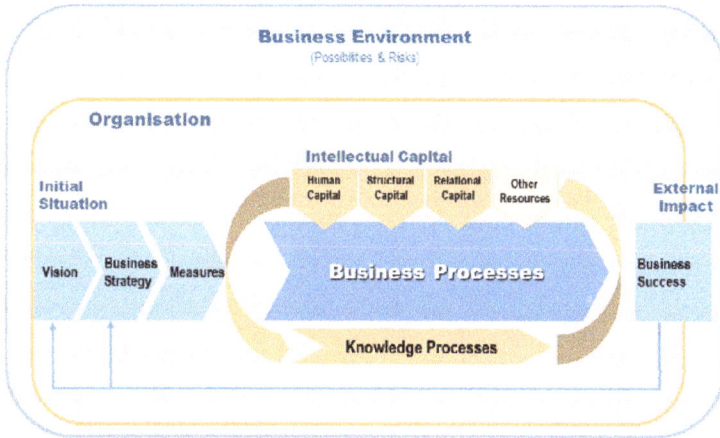

Figure 1: The ICS structural model

The German and European ICS approach consists of a procedural model to guide and to enable the ICS implementation process in a structured workshop setting.

The procedural model (see

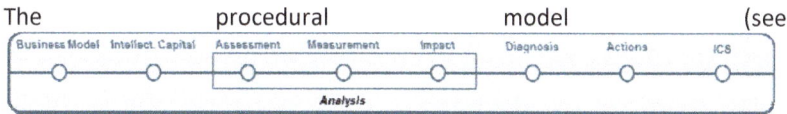

Figure 2) defines and describes eight steps as well as methodologies applied while going through the process of ICS implementation in detail (Mertins et al., 2009). It starts with the formulation of the company's business model, seeking to align IC with significant value-generating processes and, crucially, with the objectives and desired business success of the

company. This information forms the basis for the other steps that complete the procedure for applying the method, ending with the establishment of the actions and indicators, summarized in an ICS as a report and as a management presentation, to be used as a management tool for monitoring the organisational change and reporting the findings of the analysis.

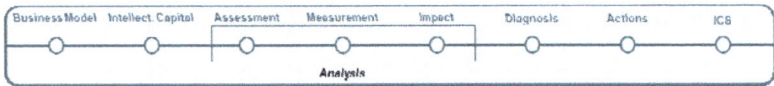

Figure 2: 8 steps of the ICS Toolbox according the ICS procedure model

The method is supported by the software "ICS Toolbox", that provides different visual forms to illustrate the results. The summarizing visualization is a portfolio of IC factors which displays the factors having the greatest impact on company results compared to their current assessment in a four quadrant matrix. The portfolio represents, on a consolidated basis, the results of the evaluation of each factor of IC. The Y axis displays the relative weight or impact of the factors on the results of the organization. The impact matrix, as a tool for analysing each factor compared to its significance in relation to the organization's results, generates this weighting measure called "relative influence". The X axis represents the consolidation of the assessment of intellectual capital factors in three dimensions: Quantity, Quality and Systematic (QQS analysis), the extent to which the company treats each of the factors. Thus, through easy and realistic illustrations, managers can manage their intangible assets and objectively assess the results over time (see Figure 3).

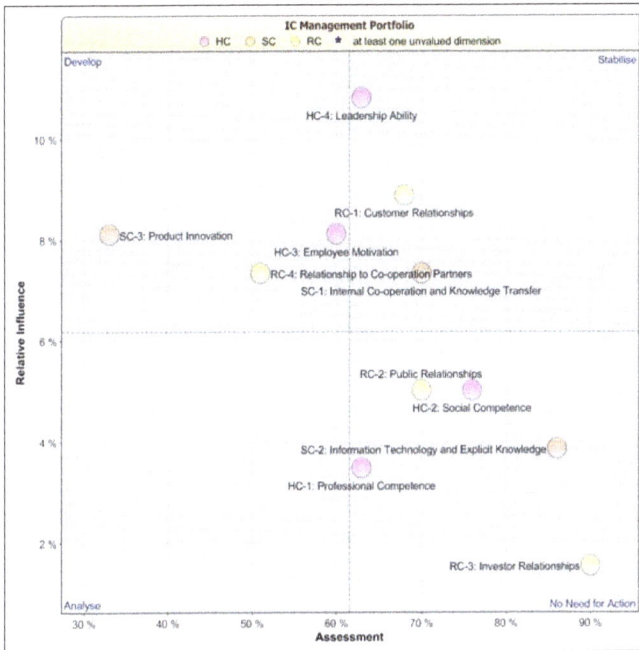

Figure 3: Example of an IC Management Portfolio

Based on this concept of defining and implementing ICS in companies, Fraunhofer IPK pushed the national IC movement forward by integrating different stakeholders and running different activities towards a "national IC Center Germany".

3 The challenges that were encountered, how they developed and how they were overcome.

Building on these learnings, Arbeitskreis Wissensbilanz could accelerate in pushing the idea of Intellectual Capital Reporting and Management to enterprises, particularly to SMEs, which are dominating the economy of German speaking countries. The requirements set by the funding institution, the German Federal Ministry for Economic Affairs were simple (Herrmann 2013):

- **Relevance**: IC as a resource needs to be leveraged in the value creation processes of enterprises. Any approach to support SMEs therefore needs to identify strategically relevant and specific drivers of Intellectual Capital. Additionally, it needs to clearly identify areas of intervention where additional financial resources might be invested in order to further develop the organization.
- **Cost efficiency**: Utilizing IC should contribute to growth and performance without creating additional burdens on corporate reporting. It should not consume scarce management resources but generate immediate returns. A priority should be the use of internal resources and expertise and only limited external support.
- **Ease of use**: the methods should emphasize simple procedures without extensive training requirements. The results should be understood as intuitively as possible in order to lower the barriers for future change and implementation of projects to improve.
- **Compatibility**: the methods applied should be compatible with already existing instruments and offer interfaces for re-use of already developed structures.

In order to accomplish these priorities, no new methods should be developed, but existing ones should be optimized and streamlined (Herrmann, 2013). Therefore, an international team of experts was formed and borrowed heavily from the experiences already made in Scandinavia and Austria. The main challenges were to develop a process that can be easily adjusted to individual SME strategy requirements and to support the process with proper tools and guidelines that serve to accelerate and to stabilize the quality of the output of the processes.

4   How the initiative was received by the users or participants.

The first experiences were made in Germany in implementing ICS on the company level and in initializing a national IC network with important stakeholders regarding IC management. Based on the development of the SME focused methodology and procedure for implementing ICS (Alwert,

2006) the very first experiences in implementing ICS in 14 pilot companies were made.

At the same time Fraunhofer developed and established a training program for ICS moderators with the aim to enable consultants and moderators in supporting companies to implement ICS according to the described procedure. Until 2006 the first 100 moderators were qualified according the first level of the training program and started further implementation in the industry.

The dissemination of the ICS concept was supported by different publications and activities. The main publication was the German ICS Guideline (FMET, 2004) where the method and procedure of implementing ICS is described in detail. Furthermore the first version of the ICS Toolbox was developed and distributed in line with the ICS Guideline. Also an image brochure was published and distributed through German companies via different events, workshops, conferences and related activities of trained ICS moderators and interested stakeholder groups to push the idea of using the ICS for internal management of SME and external communication of their IC. Until 2006 the first 9 regional ICS roadshows where organized with more than 250 participants.

The second phase of the IC movement in Germany was also funded by the Federal Ministry of Economics and Technology (FMET) in different projects with the main focus to transfer the ICS method which was developed at Fraunhofer during the first ICS pilot project into practical use. The following project should be mentioned as part of the ICS roll-out movement in Germany:

Project "ICS Roadshows": The main objective of the project "ICS Roadshows" was to raise the awareness among interested companies. As a main result within the project more than 100 roadshows with more than 4.000 visitors were carried out successfully (Glöckner 2013).

Project "ICS and quality management": The objective was to integrate the concept of ICS into the concept of quality management. The project tested

ICS implementation in companies using also a quality management system (see www.qmundwissen.de).

Project "ICS as part of external reporting": The project aimed on connecting the concept of ICS to the field of external reporting rules. As a result companies were tested using ICS in the context of external reporting leading to a special guideline using ICS in this specific context of external reporting (see http://www.wiwi.tu-claus-hal.de/abteilungen/unternehmensrechnung/forschung/drittmittelprojekte /).

Project "IC Future Check": The tool box "IC Future Check" has been developed and tested in cooperation with financial institutions and businesses within this project. The "IC Future Check" developed based on the first pilot project systematically supports the communication between bank and business and increases the transparency of intangibles (Wuscher et al., 2014). In a case study the practical use of the "IC Future Check" is demonstrated in the credit lending process.

Project "Intellectual Capital – Made in Germany": As a continuation of the first pilot project until 2006 the targets of this project were

- to increase the public attention of the ICS method, by informing the publicity via conferences, online and print media with best practices and reaching more than 5 Mio people,
- to sensitise the publicity with transparent information and offers like a newsletter with more than 3000 subscribers, launching a ICS quick-check (http://www.wissensbilanz-schnelltest.de/home) as a basis for a German IC study (Mertins et al., 2011),
- to implement more ICS in SME and develop additional modules of IC management and quality assurance, and
- to manage the different project activities and stakeholders with the aim to put all results of the funding activities from FMET into a sustainable IC movement.

Sven Wuscher, Manfred Borneman, Erik Steinhöfel, Ronald Orth

In the field of "quality assurance" additional 150 ICS moderators were trained by the Fraunhofer Academy from 2007 -2010. On the "implementation" side within this phase all project partners estimated more than 1.000 ICS implementations in Germany. Beside the training program the concept of ICS Audit was developed to ensure the implementation quality of ICS conducted by ICS moderators and to support the acceptance of the method by external stakeholders like investors or customers of companies using ICS (Wang, 2012).

Additionally the ICS Guideline (Alwert, 2013) and the ICS Toolbox were revised based on the project experiences mentioned above and developments of additional modules like the ICS Audit (Wang, 2012), the IC Benchmarking (Kohl et al., 2013) and additional guidelines connected to the ICS method. The additional guideline "Developing Strategic Goals" (Alwert, Will, 2014) shows companies how to identify their overarching corporate aims and objectives, and how to plan the strategic direction in a structured way with participation of key figures in the company. The supplementary guideline on "Management of Measures" (Alwert and Will, 2014) is focused on the planning, realisation and controlling of measures derived from ICS. On the interface of measures implementation the Intellectual Capital Statement can be used as an instrument to control transformative measures as it periodically assesses the key factors of success such as competence, structures and external relations. The changes which thus become visible offer information about the success of the measures initiated. The third new supplementary guideline "Continuous Intellectual Capital Reporting" (Alwert and Wuscher, 2014) highlights the changes that have taken place in the execution of the project since the time when the first ICS was made. With a view to controlling and, if necessary, realigning the continual review of the business model and the success of the measures initiated in the context of the ICS, this guideline recommends regular repetition of ICS implementation.

5 The outcomes that were achieved and how they were measured and evaluated.

As part of the research project, both, the software and the guideline were evaluated by project participants. Their feedback was overwhelmingly positive and lead to additional funding by the Federal Ministry as the project host (Herrmann 2013).

Another indicator for the competitiveness are recommendations by the influential association of tax advisors DATEV.ev, who support their 20.000 members with up to date tools. With three dedicated articles[1], the method was introduced to the consulting market and should be established as a standard tool. Similar support comes from International Controller Association (6.000 members in Germany, Austria and Switzerland) as an original partner (Blachfellner et al. 2007).

6 Plans to further development of the initiative.

Beside the function of further development and transfer of the IC method, Fraunhofer also had the mission to manage the different project activities and stakeholders during and after the roll-out phase with the aim to put all results of the funding activities from FMET into a sustainable IC movement.

In 2015 the German IC Center consist of different elements which have certain functions to cover the idea of increase the implementation rate of ICS in companies and ensuring a high quality of implementation as well as further developments of the method.

---

[1] DATEV Magazine: 3-2012, p. 58f; 6-2012 p 49f and 6-2015 forthcoming.

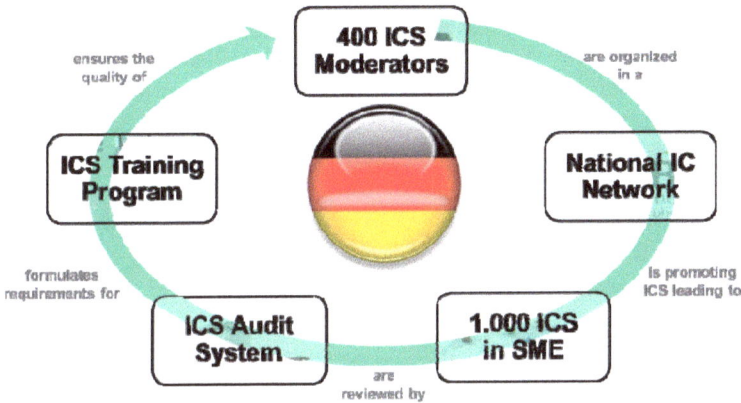

Figure 4: The German IC Center

The Fraunhofer Academy trained additional 150 ICS moderators since 2010 so that the national IC movement consists actually of 400 trained ICS moderators. Part of the moderators, interested stakeholder groups and researchers founded the registered "National Association on Intellectual Capital Management (BVWB)" in May 2012 (see http://www.bvwb.de). The BVWB as national IC network delivers the collaboration and the exchange of experiences by the members and support dissemination activities like organizing ICS roadshows, publishing information material and stimulate the continuously implementation of ICS in companies. The IC audit system is one crucial module in order to establish the ICS as part of external reporting and as an input for quality assurance of training and developments of the method. Actual discussion within the national IC Center are topics like "IC and integrated reporting" (Orth and Kohl, 2012), "IC and sustainability" (Mertins and Orth, 2012) as well as the examination of an integrated IC-Monitoring system, were the national IC Center not only investigates the IC on the company level (micro) but also on the regional and national level (Kohl et al., 2013).

First pilot projects to transfer the ICS method from German to other countries were made within the InCaS project in France, Spain, Poland and Slovenia in 2008. Also first pilot project started in Brazil in 2009 (Sequeira, 2014) and in Malaysia 2013 (AIM, 2013). The challenge of all these countries is to start the second phase of pushing the adapted ICS method to a wide national application and towards a sustainable national IC Center. The most important resources which are needed to move on in these and also in other countries is to have a national funding not only for the first pilot project but also for the crucial second rout-out phase.

References

AIM Agensi Inovasi Malaysia (2013) Anual Report 2013, pp.45 [online], http://innovation.my/wp/wp-content/uploads/2014/12/AIM2013_AR.pdf

Alwert, Kay; Will, Markus (2014): Leitfaden Maßnahmen managen. Zusatzmodul zum Leitfaden 2.0 zur Erstellung einer Wissensbilanz. Stuttgart: Fraunhofer Verlag.

Alwert, K. and Will, M. (2014): Leitfaden Maßnahmen managen. Zusatzmodul zum Leitfaden 2.0 zur Erstellung einer Wissensbilanz. Stuttgart: Fraunhofer Verlag.

Alwert, K. and Wuscher, S. (2014): Leitfaden Kontinuierliche Wissensbilanzierung. Zusatzmodul zum Leitfaden 2.0 zur Erstellung einer Wissensbilanz. Stuttgart: Fraunhofer Verlag.

Alwert, K., Bornemann, M., Will, M. and Wuscher, S. (2013): Wissensbilanz - Made in Germany. Leitfaden 2.0 zur Erstellung einer Wissensbilanz. (Ed.) Bundesministerium für Wirtschaft und Technologie. Berlin.

Alwert, K.; Bornemann, M.; Will, M. (2009): Does Intellectual Capital Reporting Matter to Financial Analysts? In Journal for intellectual Capital 2009 Emerald Group Publishing Limited ISSN 1469-1930.

Alwert, Kay; Bornemann, Manfred; Will, Markus (2008): Wissensbilanz - Made in Germany. Leitfaden 2.0 zur Erstellung einer Wissensbilanz. Hrsg. durch das Bundesministerium für Wirtschaft und Technologie. Berlin. http://www.akwissensbilanz.org/Infoservice/Infomaterial/WB-Leitfaden_2.0.pdf.

Alwert, K. (2006): Wissensbilanzen für mittelständische Organisationen. Fraunhofer IRB Verlag, Stuttgart.

Bornemann, M. Reinhardt, R. (2008): Handbuch Wissensbilanz – Umsetzung und Fallbeispiele. ESV.

Bornemann M.; Alwert, K. (2007): The German Guideline for Intellectual Capital Reporting, Journal for Intellectual capital.

Bornemann, M., Blachfellner, M.: Praxisstudie zum Thema Management von Intangibles. In: Matzler, K.; Hinterhuber, H.; Renzl B. und Rothenberger S.: Immaterielle Vermögenswerte: Handbuch der intangible Assets. ESV, November 2005.

Bornemann, Manfred; Sammer, Martin (Hg.) (2002): Anwendungsorientiertes Wissensmanagement. Ansätze und Fallstudien aus der betrieblichen und der universitären Praxis. Wiesbaden: DUV/ Gabler.

Bontis, N. (1999): Managing organizational knowledge by diagnosing intellectual capital: framing and advancing the state of the field, International Journal of Technology Management, Vol. 18 Nos. 5/6/7/8, pp. 433-62.

Danish Agency for Trade and Industry (2000): A guideline for intellectual capital statements. A key to knowledge management. Copenhagen.

Drucker, P. (1991): "The new productivity challenge", Harvard Business Review, November-December, pp. 69-79.

Edvinsson, L. and Malone, M. S. (1997): Intellectual Capital: Realizing Your Company's True Value by Finding Its Hidden Brainpower, Harper Business, New York.

European Commission (2008) InCas: Intellectual Capital Statement – Made in Europe: The ICS Guideline.

FMET - Federal Ministry of Economics and Labour (2004), Intellectual Capital Statement – Made in Germany, Berlin.

Glöckner, G. (2013) Roadshow Wissensbilanz – eine Erfolgsstory. AWF Informationen, [online] http://www.awv-net.de/cms/upload/awv-info/Info-1-13-Roadshow-WB.pdf

Guthrie, J. (2001): The management, measurement and the reporting of intellectual capital, Journal of Intellectual Capital, Vol. 2 No. 1, pp. 27-41.

Herrman, H.-J., (2013): 10 Jahre "Wissensbilanz - Made in Germany" - Stand und Perspektiven. In T. M. Fischer & I. Wulf, Wissensbilanzen im Mittelstand - Kapitalmarktkommunikation, Immaterielle Werte, Lageberichterstattung, Integrated Reporting, XBRL (S. 1-15). Stuttgart: Schäffer-Poeschel-Verlag.

Hörmann, F. (2007); Wissensbilanzen für Universitäten? Teil 1: Welche Probleme und Modellkonzeptionen bildeten den Ausgangspunkt der Entwicklung der sogenannten „Wissensbilanz" und mit welchen Methoden wurden diese Ansätze erarbeitet?. Österreichische Zeitschrift für Recht und Rechnungswesen (RWZ) (7/8): S. 211-215.

Hörmann, F. (2007): Wissensbilanzen für Universitäten? Teil 2: Welcher Aufwand bzw Nutzen kann von der übereilten Einführung eines in Erprobung befindlichen Berichtsmodells an den Universitäten erwartet werden?. Österreichische Zeitschrift für Recht und Rechnungswesen (RWZ) (11): S. 333-338.

Intellectual Capital Statement Made in Europe (2008): Project within the Sixth Research Framework Programme of the EU (FP 6) and co-financed by the European Union. See www.InCaS-europe.org

Kaplan, R.S.; Norton, D.P. (1992): The Balanced Scorecard – Measures that Drive Performance. In: Harvard Business Review. Januar–Februar 1992, P. 71–79.

Kohl, H., Orth, R., Wuscher, S. and Will, M. (2013): Challenges for an Inte-grated IC-based Monitoring System: a multi-stakeholder perspective. In: Schiuma, G.; Spender, J.; Yigitcanlar, T. (Ed.): Smart Growth: Or-ganizations, Cities and Communities. Proceedings E-Book of the In-ternational Forum on the 8th Knowledge Asset Dynamics (IFKAD). Zagreb, Croatia, 12.-14. Juni 2013, pp. 1498-1508.

Leitner, Karl-Heinz (2005): Wissensbilanzierungen für den Forschungsbereich: Erfahrungen der Austrian Research Centers. In: Kai Mertins, Kay Alwert und Peter Heisig (Hg.): Wissensbilanzen. Intellektuelles Kapital erfolgreich nutzen und entwickeln. Berlin: Springer, S. 203-224.

McGregor, D. (1960): The Human Side of Enterprise, New York, McGrawHill.

Mertins, K. and Orth, R. (2012) Intellectual Capital and the Triple Bottom Line. Overview, Concepts and Requirements for an Integrated Sus-tainability Management System. In: Surakka, J. (Ed.): Proceedings of the 4th European Conference on Intellectual Capital. Arcada Univer-sity of Applied Sciences Helsinki, Finland, 23.-24. April 2012. Reading: Academic Publishing International Ltd., S. 516-526.

Mertins, K., Will, M. and Wuscher, S. (2011): Germany - Towards a knowledge-based economy. In: Lehner, F.; Bredl, K. (Ed.): Proceedings of the 12th European Conferences on Knowledge Management. University of Passau, Germany, 1.-2. September 2011. Reading: Academic Publishing Ltd., S. 626-636.

Mertins, Kai; Will, Markus; Meyer, Cornelia (2009): InCas: Intellectual Capital Statement. Measuring Intellectual Capital in European Small and Medium sized Enterprises. In: Christiaan Stam (Hg.): Proceedings of the European Conference on Intellectual Capital (ECIC). INHolland University of Applied Sciences, Haarlem, The Netherlands, 28.-29. April 2009. Reading: Academic Publishing Ltd., S. 355-362.

Mouritsen, J. (1998): Driving growth: economic value added versus intellectual capital, Management Accounting Research, Vol. 9, pp. 461-82.

Nonaka, I. (1991): The knowledge-creating company, Harvard Business Review, November- December.

OECD (1999): International Symposium Measuring and Reporting: Intellectual Capital: Experiences, Issues and Prospects, Amsterdam, 9 June 1999

OECD (1996): The Knowledge-Based Economy; http://www.oecd.org/sti/sci-tech/1913021.pdf

Orth, R. and Kohl, H. (2012): Intellectual Capital and Sustainability Management. Perspectives for an Integrated Reporting and Benchmarking. In: Schiuma, G.; Spender, J.; Yigitcanlar, T. (Ed.) Knowledge, Innovation and Sustainability: Intergrating micro and macro perspectives. Proceedings E-Book of the International Forum on the 7th Knowledge Asset Dynamics (IFKAD) and 5th Knowledge Cities World Summit (KCWS) Joint Conference. Matera, Italy, 13.-15. June 2012, S. 159-179.

Petty, Richard; Guthrie, James (2000): Intellectual capital literature review : measurement, reporting and management. In: Journal of Intellectual Capital 1 (2), S. 155-176.

Reinhardt, R. Bornemann, M., Pawlowsky, P., Schneider, U. (2001): Intellectual Capital and Knowledge Management: Perspectives on Measuring Knowledge. In: Nonaka, I. et al, Handbook of Organizational Knowledge and Learning. Oxford.

Sammer, M.; Denscher, G. Bornemann, M. Horvath, W, (2003): Wie man das intellektuelle Kapital steuert - die Entwicklung einer

Wissensbilanz der Böhler Schmiedetechnik GmbH & Co KG. in: New Management P 62-68.

Sequeira, C. A., Will, M. and Fernández y Fernandez, E., (2014): Innovating Management or Managing Innovation, What Matters for the Brazilian SMEs? In: Vivas, C.; Sequeira, P. (Ed.): Proceedings of the 15th European Conference on Knowledge Management (ECKM). School of Management and Technology, Polytechnic Institute of Santarém, Portugal, 4-5 September 2014. Reading: Academic Conferences and Publishing International Limited, pp. 874-878.

Stewart, T.A. (1997): Intellectual Capital: The New Wealth of Organizations, Nicholas Brealey Publishing, London.

Sveiby, K.E. (1997): The New Organizational Wealth: Managing and Measuring Knowledge-based Assets, Berrett-Koehler Publishers, San Francisco, CA.

Titscher, S. Winckler, G. Biedermann, H. et al (2000): Universitäten im Wettbewerb. Zur Neustrukturierung österreichischer Universitäten. München und Mering.

Wang, W.-H. (2012): Auditierung von Wissensbilanzen. Eine Methode zur Qualitätssicherung von Bilanzen des Intellektuellen Kapitals. Stuttgart: Fraunhofer Verlag

Wuscher, S., Will, M.; Alwert, K.; Bornemann, M.: Projektstudie: Weiche Faktoren als Teil der Unternehmenseinschätzung. Studie des Fraunhofer IPK im Auftrag des BMWI, Berlin 2006. (*www.akwissensbilanz.org*)

Wuscher, S., Kohl, H. and Orth, R. (2014) IC Future Check: Greater Transparency Within the Credit Process. In: Cagáňová, D.; Čambál, M. (Ed.): Proceedings of the 6th European Conference on Intellectual Capital (ECIC). Reading: Academic Conferences and Publishing International Limited, pp. 336-341.

Will, M.; Alwert, K.; Bornemann, M.; Wuscher, S.: Auswirkungen eines Berichts über Intellektuelles Kapital auf die Unternehmensbewertung. Studie des Fraunhofer IPK im Auftrag des BMWI, Berlin 2007. (www.akwissensbilanz.org)

Whittington, R. (2001): What is Strategy- and does it matter? (2nd ed.). London: Thomson Learning.

www.ingramcontent.com/pod-product-compliance
Lightning Source LLC
Chambersburg PA
CBHW042315210326
41599CB00038B/7131